Walter Gibson's
BIG BOOK OF MAGIC
FOR ALL AGES

Walter Gibson's
BIG BOOK OF MAGIC FOR ALL AGES

*With over 150 easy-to-perform
tricks using everyday objects*

ILLUSTRATIONS BY
RIC ESTRADA

DOUBLEDAY & COMPANY, INC.
GARDEN CITY, NEW YORK

ISBN 0-385-14808-9
Library of Congress Catalog Card Number 80–496
Copyright © 1980 by Walter Gibson
Printed in the United States of America

Contents

Introduction   vii

CHAPTER ONE: How to Create a Simple Yet Challenging Act   1

CHAPTER TWO: The Performance: Presenting a Complete Act   5

CHAPTER THREE: Tricks with Rope, String, and Handkerchiefs   13
Introduction: Harry Blackstone

CHAPTER FOUR: Dinner-table Magic   39
Introduction: T. Nelson Downs

CHAPTER FIVE: Bafflers and Participation Tricks   63
Introduction: Harry Houdini

CHAPTER SIX: Mental Magic and Messages   91
Introduction: Joseph Dunninger

CHAPTER SEVEN: Money Magic   111
Introduction: Horace Goldin

CHAPTER EIGHT: Tricks with Cards   143
Introduction: Cardini

CHAPTER NINE: A Hatful of Miscellaneous Tricks   187
Introduction: The Great Raymond

CHAPTER TEN: Special Tricks for a Complete Act   219
Introduction: Howard Thurston

Introduction

MAGIC IS AN ARTFORM that is enjoyed by everyone—from the smallest child, whose entire world is magical and fantastic, to the oldest member of the family. Here is an entertaining, as well as instructional, book of tricks you can perform for all your friends and family.

Because magic is such a popular form of theater, and because all of us secretly wish we could make predictions, double our money, make objects vanish, or read someone's mind, I have collected and created an array of easily learned tricks and special effects, performed simply by using some of the most common and available items you would find in your home. There's no need for expensive equipment or devastating setups. These exciting and mystical tricks can be created with the use of plastic cups, safety pins, paper, scissors, rubber bands, pencils, handkerchiefs, matches, cards, and mental powers!

This is a book you can grow up with; there are simple tricks that a three-year-old can perform and enjoy, and there are special effects that will dazzle the most sophisticated audience.

So put on your top hat, polish your crystal ball, freshen up your white gloves, and dust off your magic wand—you are about to become a Master of Mysticism in no time at all!

CHAPTER ONE: How to Create a Simple Yet Challenging Act

THE BEST WAY to learn magic is to actually start doing magic.

This may come as a surprise to people who think that magic depends on skill and long practice. Quick moves that deceive the eye, or secret gadgets that produce incredible results, or even mystic words like "presto," "abracadabra," and "alagazam" can hold spectators spellbound. All such factors play their part in magic by creating an atmosphere of mystery or drawing the audience's attention away from the trickery. All these techniques add to the fun, both for you, as the magician, and for your audience.

Magic can be learned trick by trick, beginning with the simplest and proceeding to the more complex. By trying out certain tricks and getting them to flow together smoothly you can gradually develop routines in which tricks follow one another in logical order; and from those, you can form a full-fledged program, adapted to your needs and skills and suited for the type of audience that is watching your performance.

All the way along, you will find yourself following certain basic rules that apply to nearly all tricks—small or large—and thereby help to improve your ability step by step. That is why magic becomes easier to do the longer you stay with it.

Every trick consists of two components: effect and method. The *effect* is what the trick looks like to the audience and therefore represents the impression that you are trying to create; while the *method* is the means that you employ to attain that result.

Always, you must talk and act out the effect as if it were real, while you are thinking in terms of the method in order to put across the deception. Magicians call this *misdirection* and the term is a good one, because it leads to the *mystification* of the spectators. That is where

1

simpler tricks have an advantage over those demanding special skill, since there is less to cover up. In short, a trick that practically works itself is ideal, especially for beginners; with these tricks all the emphasis can be put on presentation.

There are two special rules that should constantly be kept in mind: One is: Be careful not to tell people exactly what you intend to do, because then they will know what to look for. By keeping the climax of the trick as a surprise, it will be difficult for observers to catch on to it in the early stages. The other rule is: Never repeat a trick on the same occasion, since that would be a violation of the previous rule, as you would be practically telling people what you intend to do.

Like all good rules, these have exceptions, which add to the fun of doing magic. With some tricks, you can tell your audience just enough to rouse their interest, without giving them the details of all that you intend to do. In fact, by emphasizing certain points, you can easily ignore others that are more important, thereby causing your audience to overlook them. As for never doing the same trick twice, there are times when you can deliberately announce that you will repeat a trick; then instead, you perform a similar effect that you have held in reserve.

This will work doubly to your advantage, because if people actually gain a clue to the first trick, they will be watching for it when you agree to do it again. Since the second trick depends on a different method, they will think they guessed wrong the first time and will be completely baffled by the repeat as well. So when you come across two or more tricks that are very similar in effect, it is a good plan to practice all of them. If you like one method better than the others, use it regularly, but be sure to have another in reserve.

When creating magic for people who have seen you do magic before, there is usually no need to worry about repeating tricks. People are apt to remember some effects to the point where they exaggerate them, so any guesses as to method will be completely wrong. But you can help that situation further by changing the order of the tricks and injecting one or two new ones as replacements so your routine will be different. This is a specially good rule if you perform before the same group often.

In choosing tricks to suit your own requirements, you should make allowance for the spectators as well, since audience reaction is a vital part of every magic show. When performing for young children, all tricks should be simple and direct, with little need for routine, except that you should hold your bigger surprises for the finish. To small children, almost anything new is somewhat magical, so you should take that approach, even with the smallest tricks. Since animation attracts the young eye, the key tricks to a good program could very well be Dicky Birds (page 192) and The Animated Hairpin (page 202), working from there up to The Animated Mouse (page 23), although this could be used in a longer program. By interspersing various simple tricks among these, you can soon judge which are most suitable for younger children, since they usually show enthusiasm for things they like best. With a group, you can always reach a climax by tearing two sheets of tissue paper and restoring them in the form of The Paper Hat (page 190), which you can replace on a child's head as a crowning achievement.

As your audiences approach the teen-age level, you will find a wide variety of appropriate tricks to choose from. All forms of money magic —coins and dollar bills—are of interest to this group, so you can follow one item with another in almost any order. The Buddha Money Mystery is a fine finale for a series of money tricks, so it is a good idea to make up a set and have it in readiness any time you expect to entertain a teen-age audience.

Since money magic is mostly performed on a table—like various other coin tricks—a transition to table magic is a logical choice. Such tricks as Balanced Egg, Magnetic Dice, Three-glass Turnup, and Turnabout Knife are specially suited to this age group.

Getting away from the table, you can baffle this same audience with tricks involving string, ropes, or handkerchiefs. It is advisable to brush up on similar tricks beforehand, such as Drop-away Knots and Go-go Knots, or Shake a Knot and Shake a Loop. This will enable you to meet the frequent demand to "do it again," which is inevitable with a young audience, and you may want to interchange these tricks quickly. If it becomes too constant, simply ignore their requests and go on with something else, like String Through Buttonhole, which is one trick you can repeat several times, leaving the youthful onlookers still befuddled.

Tricks described under Puzzlers rouse the interest of this group, and the tricks involving a partner are among the best, particularly if you use a member of the audience to help you. Using someone from the audience requires some secret coaching beforehand, which is usually quite easy to arrange.

Any of the Do as I Do effects have a strong appeal to teen-age spectators, since they will get a chance to participate in the tricks—always a delight for more youthful onlookers.

Once you have performed for a group of teen-agers, the tricks you will be doing will have practically reached the adult level. You can now discard the simpler or more elementary tricks, except when they can be casually dropped in at some point during your routine.

Card tricks and mental magic come to the forefront with both teen-agers and adults, because these tricks demand concentration and provide a challenge that is beyond the limitations of younger audiences.

An excellent opening effect is Link the Pins, described under Miscellaneous Tricks, because it requires special preparation and therefore must be in readiness at the very start. It also gives you the advantage of a good follow-up in Take-apart Pins. Another pair of tricks, The Climbing Ring and The Rising Pencil, can also be used in tandem as a starter, since they too depend upon advance preparation.

Leading from one trick to another is always good with this type of audience; for example, under Table Magic, Three-glass Turnup is always good until too many people start trying it for themselves, so at that point you can switch to Five in a Row and present them with a still more puzzling problem.

Any knot tricks—whether with string, rope, or handkerchiefs—will keep your audience guessing when you switch from one to another. But you may find that tricks of mental magic will be your best standby.

With mental magic you may find teen-agers just as alert as adults and sometimes even more so. Teen-agers are also more outspoken, but don't let that bother you. Just keep your presentation moving. There are times when your audience may guess the answer correctly, but often they don't realize it, so if you smile and proceed with your next trick they are apt to wind up thinking they were wrong.

Always refer to a mental effect as a "test" rather than a "trick," so if you fail once, you will have the right to try again and when you succeed, people are apt to think it is something more than magic, like extrasensory perception.

Card tricks, particularly the dealing type, can be interwoven with mental magic, adding to the effectiveness of both. Card tricks can also be performed as an act all by themselves, which is very impressive especially when you use a borrowed pack.

Experiment, and you will eventually develop an act that is comfortable for you. It is important that your tricks fit your skill and your personality, in order for you to perform well.

CHAPTER TWO: The Performance: Presenting a Complete Act

ONCE YOU HAVE developed a few individual routines, particularly those suited to a sizable audience, you will be on your way toward presenting a complete magic act. As you progress you will have the choice of working "single"—that is, doing the act all by yourself—or putting on a "double" act, using an assistant. The choice of doing a single or a double act is often a matter of convenience. Some noted magicians—T. Nelson Downs, for example—have always worked entirely alone; while others, like Thurston and Cardini, used an assistant almost from the start. The exception to both rules was Jarrow, who found that theaters would pay more for a double act than a single, so he booked himself as Jarrow and Johnson; but for various reasons his partner, Johnson, never appeared, so Jarrow had to do all his tricks for Johnson and collect the double salary as well.

For practical purposes, it is best to work alone in the beginning, in order to decide just when and why an assistant will be needed as you improve or expand your act. You can then assign certain duties to a helper, limiting them to minor details that almost anyone could handle. Then, as the need for an assistant increases, you can take a regular helper into your confidence, so that he or she can become an integral part of your act. It is advisable to have a substitute available for occasions when your regular assistant may not be available.

To add polish to your act, you might want to wear something mystical-looking; a homemade top hat and cape always give an air of magic, while a bright flower in a lapel or a colorful handkerchief can add to your onstage appearance. Whatever is comfortable and won't get in the way is suitable for performing magic.

After you've tested out enough tricks, you will have the framework for a complete act that you can build on. As a working example of how an act can be established and expanded, the following program is composed chiefly of special effects that will appeal to advanced performers, as well as those who are still trying out comparatively simple routines. This example shows how an act should be built to provide variety while rising to a climax, yet at the same time suited to the style of the individual performer. From there, the act will be expanded, moving you from a single into a double presentation.

6

This act follows a standard pattern, consisting of three phases: An *opening*, which should be a trick that is simple, yet surprising. From that, you move into a *sequence* of effects, which have some connection, whether real or imaginary, so that they follow one another in somewhat logical order, increasing the audience's interest on to the *finale*, which marks the finish of the act. The basic program runs as follows:

1. Tick-Tack-Toe
2. Tri-cut Rope
3. The Bottle Imp
4. The Oriental Snowstorm
5. Silly Spooks
6. The Inexhaustible Box

To prepare your act, you would need a table set up with your equipment before you start. A card table will serve this purpose, but sometimes a smaller table might be better. Some professional magicians use tables with tops that are only fifteen inches square, which is just one quarter the size of a standard card table. Small side stands are therefore added to the setup, so that the performer can work from the center table, laying articles on the side stands as he finishes with them.

If you use a card table for your center piece, you can place two chairs alongside. Then, referring to your program, proceed to set up your act as follows:

1. At front of table, place sheet of paper marked with X's and O's for Tick-Tack-Toe (See page 68), with large scissors beside it.

2. At left front, lay rope for Tri-cut Rope (See page 38), either bunched together or formed in a loose coil.

3. At right of table, the bottle for The Bottle Imp (See page 197), with the little ball inside it.

4. Behind rope, put packet of paper flakes for The Oriental Snowstorm (See page 228), covered by a small sheet of thin paper. Beside it, a glass of water and a fan.

5. At back, the cloth for Silly Spooks (See page 225), with items needed for the trick: bell, ruler, etc.

6. On chair at right, The Inexhaustible Box (See page 230), fully loaded, with cardboard square on top.

In a large, ample room, arrange your "stage set" at one end, keeping spectators directly in front of you to avoid bad angles. If cramped for space set up your stage in a corner of the room, which automatically solves the angle problem. Two rooms with a connecting archway are ideal, as you can put your audience in one and use the other for your stage. The same applies with a big room separated by a room divider or curtain. It would be ideal if you could stretch a curtain between your stage and the audience; that way you keep the audience in an expectant mood while you are setting up your act and then you can make a more spectacular appearance when the curtain is drawn wide. If you use a curtain, remember to arrange for someone to open and close it at the start and finish of your act, rather than try to do it yourself. It might be a good idea to have a dark curtain or wall behind you, especially when illusion or disappearance is part of your act.

From the moment that you face your audience, you should adopt a certain style suited to your own personality and the type of tricks you are performing. Your talk or "patter" is a very important aspect of your act, as it often enables you to put across your deceptions in an unsuspected manner. The patter should be rehearsed along with tricks, as there are always times when you will be talking about one thing and doing something else. The same applies to gestures and other actions that accompany your patter.

There are three styles of presentation popular with experienced magicians, and often a performer concentrates on the type that he likes best or that seems most suited to his audience. However, in forming an act, it is a good plan to adopt all three, since each has its advantages with certain tricks, and by switching from one to another, you can change your pace and avoid repetition. The three styles are the *humorous*, in which you treat your tricks lightly, almost flippantly, as though inviting your audience to join in the fun; the *serious*, where you treat a trick like a scientific experiment; and the *mysterious*, which takes on the semblance of real magic.

A humorous style puts an audience in a good mood, but too much fast talk can become tiring, so it is better to adopt a serious style as the act progresses, injecting a few appropriate quips at intervals. Whenever you are short of talk, you can adopt the mysterious style, using gestures more than patter; and it is here that musical accompaniment can figure strongly, as it will enable you to work silently, with all the emphasis on your magic. Record appropriate music on a cassette. Instruct someone as to when to start the tape during the course of your performance. It will add a fine touch to the entire presentation.

When opening your act with the humorous approach, you might bow to your audience and begin your patter along the following line: "Before I deceive you with some mysteries of modern magic, let me assure you that I have nothing up my sleeves except my arms." Here, you draw up one sleeve, then the other, and spread your hands, adding: "Also note that my hands are completely empty and not for a moment will they ever leave my wrists. In fact, I am very strongly attached to my hands, because I have had them ever since I can remember." Turning to the table, pick up the tick-tack-toe sheet and the scissors and approach a spectator, saying:

"Let's start with a magic game of Tick-Tack-Toe. Look at this sheet of paper and tell me which you want, the X's or the O's." If he chooses the X's, hand him the scissors and tell him to hold them point upward and open them so they form a letter X. Have him keep staring steadily at the scissors, while you fold the paper along the creased lines; then take the scissors, clip the folded paper, hand him the X portion, and say: "There are your X's and that leaves me the O's." Spreading the O portion, you add: "Marvelous, wasn't it!"

If he should choose the O's, hand him the scissors, point downward, and tell him to keep staring at the two handles, each representing a letter O. Fold the paper, clip it, and give him the O portion, keeping the X portion for yourself. Either way, it works just the same!

Now, adopting a serious mood, take all the cut papers in your left hand and hold the scissors in your right, saying, "The whole secret is in the scissors. They are magic scissors and I will show you why!" Turn to the table, place the cut papers on the sheet that covers the packet for The Oriental Snowstorm, and pick up the coiled rope with your right hand. Turn to the audience and perform the Tri-cut Rope, stating that although the scissors seem to cut the rope, the result is only temporary. Winding the rope around one hand, steal the knots with the other and reach in your pocket for some "invisible powder," leaving the knots there. Make a big production out of sprinkling the rope with the imaginary powder and then show the rope intact.

Using the same rope, pick up the bottle and perform The Bottle Imp, treating it humorously or seriously, whichever you prefer. As you finish the trick, form the rope into a round coil and set it on the table; then pick up the torn papers from the Tick-Tack-Toe, along with the sheet of paper and the hidden packet containing the flakes for The Oriental Snowstorm. Here you assume a mysterious manner, announcing that you will present a miracle made famous in the mystic land of Tibet, where wizards can conjure up rain, hail, and even snowstorms by merely soaking strips of paper in water and fanning them into life. Now dip the papers in the glass of water and proceed.

Here is a good place to inject some music, which could be a tinkly oriental tune, or something on the order of sleigh bells. Even without music, very little patter is necessary as the fluttering paper flakes practically speak for themselves. At the finish, you can take a bow as though you were the Grand Lama in person. When you lay down the fan, you can set it directly on the coiled rope, letting the wad of soaked papers drop into the coil itself, which makes a very neat getaway.

Now let the music keep running into a weird, spooky tune, as you gather items that you have already used and place them on the chair at the left, thus clearing the table for Silly Spooks. The wadded papers can be gathered within the coiled rope as you take it from the table, thus being removed unnoticed. Continuing your mysterious tone, you state that the spirits of the Western world are just as remarkable as the mystics of the Far East; and to prove it, you go through with your spook show, taking another bow at the finish.

That brings you to the grand finale. After putting the cloth and other items used in Silly Spooks on the chair at the left, step across and bring The Inexhaustible Box from the chair on the right, placing it on the cleared table. After showing the box empty, begin producing the hidden contents and spreading them around the box. Again, music is effective here. A good spirited tune can be substituted for patter as you proceed with producing item after item. At the finish, you can gather all the loose articles and drop them in the box, along with the items used earlier, showing that they more than fill the box and thus adding to the climax.

An assistant should be an aid to you, the performer, making it possible for you to create more magic with ease. It is essential to practice with your assistant many times so that everything will run smoothly. Your assistant should know your cues and should make things less confusing for you and the audience. An assistant may serve as a needed distraction at times, but should never overpower you or the magic.

When working with an assistant, you should increase the scope of your act as far as possible. Instead of having everything set up on your table, you can have your assistant bring out various tricks and take away others. This speeds up the act and enables you to include special effects. Your assistant can handle the cassette or tape recorder, thus providing a continuous musical score. And the assistant can handle any special sound effects. Most important, however, is your stage set. It must have "wings" so that your assistant can come on and off the set as required.

If you are working in a large room with an archway, your problem is already solved, but if you are in a single room, some other provision must be made. If a folding screen is available, stand it to the right of your table, allowing space behind the screen for another table or some chairs, where your assistant can handle the various props that are used in the act. Instead of a screen, you can hang a small curtain or drape across the corner of the room to serve that purpose. If you decide to use a front curtain, stretched across the room, you won't need a screen or corner drape. Your assistant simply sets his props to the right; and to start the act, he only opens the curtain partway, thus keeping his own setup out of view.

If you are using an assistant, you can add two specific effects to your program. One is The Vanishing Bowl (See page 226), which, when referring back to the original program list, should be listed as "3-A," since it follows The Bottle Imp. The other is Ball and Rope (See page 227), which would be "4-A," coming just after The Oriental Snowstorm. In setting up your own table, all you need are these items: Paper and scissors for Tick-Tack-Toe; the packet of paper flakes for The Oriental Snowstorm, which is set behind the bowl to be used in The Vanishing Bowl. The bowl itself contains just enough water to fill an empty glass, which is standing beside it, with the fan also there. Everything else, including the tray for The Vanishing Bowl, is out of sight on your assistant's "prop" table. The tray is to be used for carrying articles on and off stage, so it will not cause suspicion when used in the bowl vanish.

Start your act with Tick-Tack-Toe and as you clip the folded paper, the assistant comes from the wing, bringing the coiled rope on the tray. This enables you to lay the scissors on the tray while you open the papers (X's and O's) and then place the papers on the tray in order to take the rope and later the scissors to perform Tri-cut Rope. The assistant stands by until you are done with the scissors and have laid them on the tray. Then, as you are finishing the rope trick, the assistant casually lays the cut papers on the packet behind the bowl and goes backstage with the tray.

There he lays the scissors aside and picks up the bottle for The Bottle Imp, putting it on the tray and bringing it onstage just as you finish restoring the rope. When you take the bottle, the assistant lowers the tray in natural fashion and walks off. After you conclude The Bottle Imp, the assistant comes on again with the tray to receive the bottle, which is carried off while you are coiling the rope and laying it on the table in readiness for The Oriental Snowstorm.

Here you inject an added touch of the mysterious. Picking up the bowl, state: "This magic bowl comes straight from the mystic land of ancient Tibet, as a special gift from the Grand Lama. It contains melted snow from the summits of the Himalaya Mountains, which I

11

will use in my next mystery." Here you pour the water from the bowl into the glass. Then add: "Since the magic bowl has now served its purpose, it must be returned to the Grand Lama's palace in the forbidden city of Lhasa."

By now your assistant has returned, bringing the tray with the cloth for the bowl trick lying on it. Lift the cloth, place the bowl on the tray, cover it, and step forward while the assistant lowers the tray and strolls offstage, while you are tossing the cloth in the air and showing that the bowl has vanished. Laying the cloth on the table, you proceed with The Oriental Snowstorm, remarking that the icy water from the Himalayas has turned the soaked paper back into the original snowflakes.

As you lay the fan on the coil of rope, the assistant comes on with Ball and Rope. This, of course, is a special rope, with a string attached, as described under Ball and Rope. You stretch the rope, the assistant puts the ball in place, and you cause the ball to run back and forth along the rope in mysterious fashion, finally catching it in one hand and showing both rope and ball to be quite ordinary. During the trick, the assistant gets the tray and gathers all the items from the table; and at the finish, you drop the ball and rope on the tray along with them. The assistant hands you the cloth for Silly Spooks and walks off with the tray.

By the time you have shown the cloth, the assistant has brought on the articles needed for Silly Spooks and stands by while you perform the trick. This enables you to inject some comedy by having the "spooks" toss articles at the assistant, who ducks away as if scared and pretends to be as amazed as the audience. The assistant finally brings on The Inexhaustible Box, which you show empty while the assistant is taking away the spooky articles, and as you start producing articles, the assistant comes on with the tray to receive them. This leads to the finale.

The act should be kept fairly flexible, to allow for any other tricks that may be inserted at different spots; and if well rehearsed, the audience is almost sure to demand an encore. So after closing the curtain, you can have the assistant reopen it and bring you two strips of paper for The Paper Hat, which you produce magically from the torn strips and place it on your assistant's head so that you both can take a final bow.

CHAPTER THREE: Tricks with Rope, String, and Handkerchiefs

Harry Blackstone

ON THE AFTERNOON OF Thursday, October 8, 1914, a brisk, personable man about thirty years old stopped by at the Magic Shop in Philadelphia to greet the members of the newly formed Mephisto Club, which was about to hold a special meeting. His name was Harry Bouton and he was appearing with his company of four assistants at the Globe Theater, just around the corner, headlining the program with a half-hour magic act.

One of the Mephisto members who had seen the show spoke so highly of Bouton's skill at card manipulation that Bouton volunteered to demonstrate it then and there. Taking six cards from a pack, Bouton vanished them one by one, at only six feet away from his audience; then he plucked them from thin air under the goggle-eyed gaze of his fellow magicians. Giving the group a parting wave, he continued on his way to get ready for his next show.

After that display of Bouton's ability, the Mephisto members could hardly wait to see his full performance. So they arranged a box party and attended in full force. The act opened with two assistants showing both sides of a four-fold screen, which they formed into a square at the very front of the stage. There was a flash of flame and smoke and out stepped the magician, wearing a devil's costume, which naturally drew applause from the Mephisto members. Discarding his satanic regalia, he became Harry Bouton in evening clothes and continued with his act, which included his card manipulation and a variety of other magical effects.

HARRY BLACKSTONE

The climax was the Bridal Chamber, an illusion involving a large skeleton cabinet (i.e. a cabinet without concealed pockets or hidden chambers), which was shown completely empty. After the two assistants drew curtains that enclosed the cabinet, the magician gave a wide sweep of his arms and the curtains were whisked away to show a complete bedroom set, with a bowing bride attired in her wedding costume and a smiling maid beside her, stroking a full-grown Russian wolfhound that had somehow wangled its way into the act.

The response from the Mephisto party was stupendous. I know, because I was a youthful member of the group. We occupied a balcony box close to the stage, and Louis Lyons, owner of the Magic Shop, had provided us with packets of artificial "spring flowers" that packed flat but opened automatically when released. There were fifty flowers to a packet, held by wire clips that broke apart when we threw them on the stage so that Harry Bouton & Company were practically bombed by miniature bouquets that sprouted all around them. A much better tribute, we thought, than ordering wreaths from a florist's shop and having ushers carry them up onto the stage.

Harry Bouton thought so, too. He told me so, when he again appeared in Philadelphia, more than eight years later. By then, he had changed his name to Blackstone and was traveling with a company of more than a dozen people. He put on a headline show at the Nixon Theater, finishing his fifty-minute act with a Vanishing Horse. Among the many new tricks that he presented was the production of hundreds of beautifully colored flowers that poured incessantly from a large sheet of cardboard, which he had shown on both sides and then formed into a cone. After the show, he told me that he was using the same flowers that Lyons and the Mephisto Club had so generously showered upon him years before. His assistants had swept them up, but instead of throwing them out, they had packed them up and taken them along for future use with the show.

That was typical of Blackstone, who was one magician who never missed a trick. All during his travels, he was acquiring everything from new costumes and new scenery to new tricks and illusions, many of which he planned while on the road and then built during the summer at his workshop in Colon, Michigan. Nearly all his time was dedicated to magic, small as well as large. He enjoyed doing card tricks for other magicians as much as he liked putting on a big illusion show for a theater audience.

Over a period of some thirty years, Blackstone and I spent days, weeks, and even months together, so I saw his show grow bigger and better, year after year. Always, Blackstone was hoping to fulfill a life-long ambition of traveling season after season with a full evening show, as Herrmann, Kellar, and Thurston had before him, but as stage shows and vaudeville gave way to talking pictures and radio, that goal seemed increasingly unattainable. Then, with the start of World War II, there was a sudden demand for live entertainment at Army and Navy bases throughout the country and abroad.

Blackstone was an immediate choice. Many servicemen had seen his show in their younger days and were eager to witness it again. Magic itself was a universal form of entertainment, so the United Service Organization promptly started Blackstone on a tour of the military bases with a full evening show that proved an immediate success. When the war ended, the theater business experienced a surprising revival, and Blackstone, by then in his early sixties, went on tour with a company of twenty to thirty people, rivalling the big shows of the past.

During 1946 and 1947, when I accompanied him on a coast-to-coast tour, Blackstone not only put on his full show, but also visited government hospitals in all the larger cities to renew acquaintance with disabled veterans who remembered him from his years with the USO, when he had invited servicemen on the stage to help with his card tricks. Now, with Blackstone working at close range in the hospitals, nearly everybody participated, and Blackstone climaxed his performances with a touch of comedy magic that really "wowed" his audiences.

Announcing that he would try an experiment in hypnotism, he had a volunteer stand facing the audience and posted another man in back to catch him in case the volunteer happened to fall. Standing at the volunteer's left, Blackstone rolled a borrowed handkerchief into a ball and gave his hands a sudden upward spread. To the man's amazement, the handkerchief was gone; and when Blackstone suddenly snatched it from nowhere, the volunteer began to believe he was really hypnotized. His wonderment increased when Blackstone repeated the procedure time and again, bringing uproarious laughter from the entire crowd of onlookers.

What Blackstone did was simply give the rolled-up handkerchief a backhand toss over the volunteer's head, where it was caught by the helper stationed behind him. While the puzzled volunteer was looking at Blackstone's empty hands and peering under his coat, Blackstone would draw his attention toward the left and would reach behind the man's back with his right hand, taking the missing handkerchief from his helper and deftly bringing it into sight.

After repeating the trick a few times with some neat variations, Blackstone would vanish the handkerchief and instead of reproducing it, he would pick up an empty drinking glass and give it a quick toss over the baffled man's head. It, too, was caught by the handy helper, who already had the handkerchief and would push it into the glass while the volunteer was wondering if both had gone up Blackstone's sleeve. This time, Blackstone would find a chance to reach behind him and recover the glass with the handkerchief inside it, bringing both from beneath his coat, or sliding them under the man's coat and producing them from there.

That sometimes concluded the routine, but quite often Blackstone would add to the comedy by picking up a pitcher full of ice water, as though about to vanish it. That was a cue for the waiting helper to throw up his hands in horror and duck away before the pitcher came flying in his direction, while the audience howled in delight—with the exception of the lone volunteer, who stood there, still wondering what it was all about. Blackstone then placed the pitcher on a table instead of tossing it and joined in the laugh.

I often played the part of Blackstone's helper, and on one occasion he was doing the trick for a group of workers just inside the open door of a fairly large garage. The door was of the flexible type that slid up along the ceiling, and Blackstone gave the handkerchief such a hefty

Quick Vanish

toss that it went high over the volunteer's head and landed on the door itself. So I had to go out and retrieve the handkerchief and get it back to Blackstone. All that while, Blackstone kept the volunteer wondering where the handkerchief could possibly be, never guessing that all the delay and commotion going on behind him had much to do with the handkerchief's vanishing and reappearance. That was real magic on Blackstone's part.

To present Quick Vanish as an absolute mystery, it should be worked as a one-person effect, with or without the aid of a helper. The "one-person" refers to a single person who serves as your audience, without any other onlookers on hand to turn a near miracle into a barrel of fun.

Seat the lone spectator in a chair and stand directly in front of him, showing a small handkerchief or a fairly large paper napkin. Roll or compress the handkerchief into a compact wad between your hands, gradually bringing them closer to the person's eyes, raising them to that level. Turn your hands sideways until the back of the left hand cuts off the view of your right palm, which is cupped so that the thumb and fingers can grip the handkerchief, with the thumb stretching across in front of it, if necessary. At this point, start moving your hands up and down, fairly rapidly, and as they go above the spectator's eye level, draw your right hand backward a few inches and thrust it just above the left. Snap your right hand forward so the heel of the right hand hits the left palm with a hard, resounding slap, spreading the right thumb and fingers sufficiently to release the wadded handkerchief.

The spectator, whose view is blocked, mistakes the loud slap for a clap of your hands, never realizing that you have driven the handkerchief on a beeline straight over his head, for it actually goes that fast. To further the deception, bring your hands toward you, like a recoil, spreading them in the same action; then actually clapping them together, now that they are far enough away for the spectator to see them. This gives the impression that you clapped your hands twice and that did it. Being positive that you must have the handkerchief somewhere on your person, your friend will never think to look elsewhere for it.

By seating the lone spectator in front of a table, you drive the handkerchief far enough to drop beyond it, leaving no evidence of where it went; and you can later reclaim it at your leisure. A low bookcase or a television set will serve just as well. Of course, you can still rely on a friend who is "in the know" to serve as a hidden helper by catching the flying object or picking it up while the baffled spectator is insisting that you open your coat or roll up your sleeves to aid the search for something that has really gone!

SHAKE A KNOT

Simple but effective, this trick catches people completely by surprise. Dangle a handkerchief by one corner from your right hand, pointing to the lower corner with your left hand (Fig. 1). The left hand raises that corner to the right, giving it a downward shake, still retaining its hold on the upper corner. This action is repeated a few times (Fig. 2), but nothing happens. However, on the final try, you give the corner a really hard shake and a knot appears instantly and magically on the lower corner! (Fig. 3).

You prepare for this surprise beforehand by secretly tying a small, tight knot in one corner of the handkerchief. When you show the handkerchief (as in Fig. 1), you keep the knot concealed between your right thumb and fingers, which are bunched to hide it. Pointing to the lower corner keeps attention centered there; and each time it is raised to the right hand, it is promptly shaken downward in natural style (as in Figs. 2 and 3)—that is, until the last time.

Then, instead of lightly holding the handkerchief in the right hand between thumb and forefinger, grip it firmly; and this time when giving the downward shake, let the knotted corner go instead (Fig. 4). The move is an absolute fooler, with the action covered by a more forcible shake, which after so many previous attempts will seem natural in itself. The result is the sudden appearance of the knot on what the onlookers still think is the lower corner.

SHAKE A LOOP

For those who have seen Shake a Knot (page 19), this effect will provide a new surprise. Instead of a knot appearing in a dangling corner of a handkerchief, two corners tie themselves together, forming a loop. Begin by dangling the handkerchief from your right thumb and fingers, casually letting people see both the upper and lower corners (Fig. 1). Then lay the handkerchief across the palm of the left hand, and with your right hand, bring one corner to the center (Fig. 2), and do the same with the other corner. Gripping the corners with your right thumb and fingers, give a downward shake and the ends of the handkerchief tie themselves into a loop! (Fig. 3).

The preparation in this case is quite artful. Spread the handkerchief on a table and bring the side corners in to the center, where you tie them together. Bunch the handkerchief loosely in your pocket, so when you bring it out, you can openly dangle it by its upper end (as in Fig. 1). Nobody suspects that the side corners of the handkerchief are already tied together, because they are out of sight behind the handkerchief (Fig. 4). When you grip the center of the handkerchief, your left fingers hide the knot while you bring the free ends together (as in Fig. 2).

Now stating that you will grip the two corners together, dip deep into the cloth with your right thumb and fingers, plucking the knotted side corners instead (Fig. 5). Raising your right hand quickly, give the handkerchief a hard downward shake, retaining your grip on the knot. By thrusting both

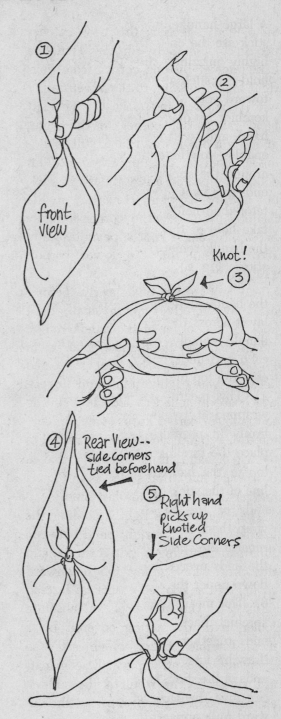

① front view

②

Knot! ③

④ Rear View -- Side corners tied beforehand

⑤ Right hand picks up knotted Side Corners

thumbs into the loop thus formed, spread it (as in Fig. 3) and display the magically knotted corners!

PENETRATING HANDKERCHIEF

A large handkerchief and a twelve-inch stick are the only items needed for this highly puzzling effect. Have someone hold the stick at one end and extend it toward you. Meanwhile, take the handkerchief by diagonal ends, one in each hand, and twist it in rope fashion. This enables you to wrap the handkerchief around the stick four times and tie the ends in a knot (Fig. 1). While the spectator then holds both ends of the stick, take hold of the knotted ends and pull the handkerchief right through the solid stick! (Fig. 2).

The secret lies in the way you wrap the handkerchief around the stick. First lay it across the stick so that both ends dangle equally (Fig. 3). Then bring each end underneath the stick, up and over the top in opposite directions (Fig. 4). This means that you have actually wrapped it twice around. To keep it firmly in position, tell your helper to place the forefinger of his free hand on top of the handkerchief, following the line of the stick (Fig. 5). Next, take the ends of the handkerchief and again wrap them around the stick, but in the *reverse direction,* so that you first carry the ends over the person's finger, then down under the stick and up over (Fig. 6). This means that you wrap the handkerchief back around twice. Tie the ends together and tell your helper to draw his finger free, so he can grip both ends of the stick. As soon as he does, you can give the handkerchief a quick upward pull, apparently right through the stick. Done properly, the reverse wrapping process nullifies the first, making

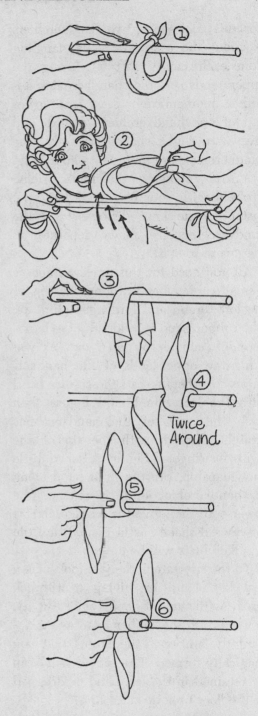

the result automatic, once the spectator withdraws his finger.

UNITED AND UNTIED

For this trick show two handkerchiefs of about the same size, one dangling from each hand (Fig. 1). Bring the upper ends of the handkerchief together momentarily, draw the lower end of one handkerchief upward, and give it a slight shake. Instantly, the handkerchiefs are united in a knot (Fig. 2). After showing the knot briefly, stroke it with your free hand (Fig. 3). Instantly, the knot dissolves and the handkerchiefs are shown separate, as they were to start.

All you need for this quick miracle is a small rubber band around the tips of the left thumb and forefinger (Fig. 4). The rubber band is hidden by the handkerchief held in the left hand. As you bring the upper ends of the handkerchiefs together, spread the rubber band with the left thumb and finger; then push the ends of the handkerchiefs straight through with the tip of the right forefinger (Fig. 5). For a little showmanship, run the right hand along its handkerchief until it reaches the lower end; then give the handkerchief a downward shake (as in Fig. 2) and the handkerchiefs will be united.

To the spectators, the join looks like a real knot, and by giving it a quick stroke with the left hand (as in Fig. 3), you can pull the rubber band away, apparently "untying" the "knot" that you magically formed. The rubber band can be retained in the left hand or dropped to the floor unnoticed.

NOTE: For close range, use two handkerchiefs of the same color with a rubber band to match, or two dark handkerchiefs with a dark rubber band.

22

THE ANIMATED MOUSE

The best way to learn this trick is to surprise yourself with it, which you can readily do by following the directions exactly. Lay a fair-sized handkerchief on the table, with a corner pointing toward you; then fold that near corner over to meet the far corner (Fig. 1).

From there, you fold in the side corners (X and X) so they come together on the center line (Fig. 2). Next, you roll the center portion—with the corners X and X—upward toward the two far corners until you reach the line indicated by the letters Y and Y. That done, lay the fingers of your right hand palm upward on the rolled-up center, pressing it down tightly (Fig. 3).

With your left hand, bring the far corners of the handkerchief downward so they cover your right fingers and fold the side ends (Z and Z) inward so that they overlap, enabling you to hold them in place with your right thumb (Fig. 4). This tucks your right fingers into a close-fitting pocket, and to retain it, you turn the handkerchief inside out with your left hand.

Both hands then work together, continuing that process until two tiny corners pop into view. One represents the head, the other the tail of the mouse (Fig. 5). By laying it on the upturned right hand and giving it a slight kick with the fingers (Fig. 6) the mouse will apparently climb the right forearm (Fig. 7). This action can be covered with the left hand, making it all the more realistic.

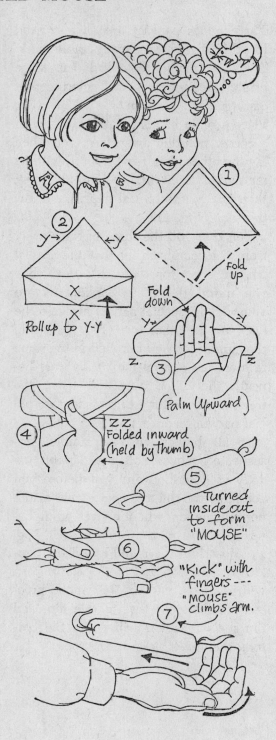

THREE PAPER NAPKINS

Three paper napkins are all you need for this highly perplexing table trick. Two are plain; the third has some printed design or special coloring that distinguishes it from the other two. Place a plain napkin on the table, with a corner pointing away from you; then lay the other plain napkin on it, with its far corner a bit higher than the first; then finally, the special napkin still farther out (Fig. 1).

You then roll the three napkins away from you, emphasizing that the special napkin is on top (Fig. 2). But when you unroll the three napkins toward yourself, the special napkin proves to be between the other two (Fig. 3). When they are rolled and unrolled in the same fashion, the special napkin appears beneath the other two; and when the process is done for a third time, the special napkin reappears on top!

It all hinges on one simple, unsuspected move. Roll the napkins exactly as described and just before you complete the roll, the near corner of the bottom napkin will flip over from beneath, ahead of the others (as in Fig. 2). Stop right there and unroll the napkins toward you and the special napkin will be in the middle. Repeat the process, watching for that telltale flip; and the special napkin will go to the bottom; then back again to the top.

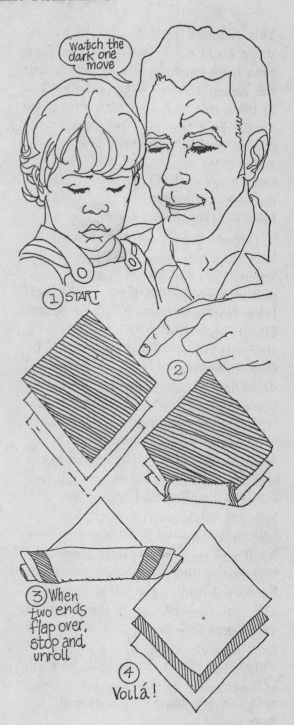

24

VANISHING KNOT

This requires a piece of fairly heavy string about three feet in length. First, tie a loose single knot in the center of the string, forming a loop about two inches across. Above that, tie a standard double knot, forming a loop equal in size to the lower. To the double knot add a third and even a fourth knot to make it stronger. Then draw the ends of the string wide apart and have somebody hold them (Fig. 1).

You now point out that to remove the knot from between the loops would be impossible, as you would either have to pull it down through the bottom of the lower loop or carry completely over the bigger knot and off the end of the string. However, you say that it can be done by making the knot invisible and dissolving it magically. To help that process, cover the center of the string with a handkerchief (Fig. 2). Then:

Reaching beneath with both hands, work on the knot briefly. For a little showmanship bring your left hand from under the cloth, pretending that you are bringing the knot with it. Being invisible, no one sees it when you open your hand and rub your thumb and fingers together to dissolve it. With your right hand, you lift away the handkerchief and to the surprise of the onlookers, the single knot is gone, leaving only a large loop instead of the two smaller ones (Fig. 3).

What really happens under the cloth is this: You spread the lower loop with both hands, working the single knot upward until it joins the big knot above (Fig. 4). By pulling the string toward

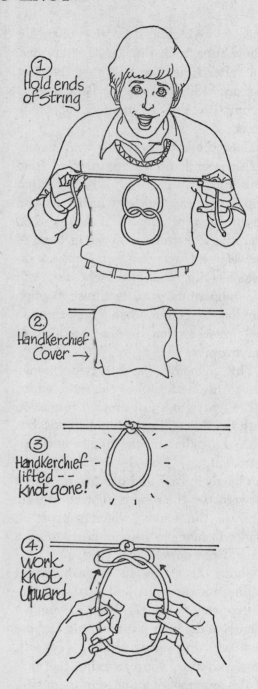

1. Hold ends of string

2. Handkerchief Cover →

3. Handkerchief lifted -- knot gone!

4. Work knot upward

the ends, the big knot is tightened and when the handkerchief is removed, the missing single knot passes as part of the big upper knot.

DROP-AWAY KNOT

This is a highly deceptive, hard-to-follow rope trick that can be repeated time after time. You will need five feet or more of heavy string or light rope to accomplish this seemingly impossible effect.

Hold the rope between your hands, with the ends protruding upward from your upright fists (Fig. 1). Keeping that grip firmly, the right fist brings its end up in front of the left forearm, then over the forearm and down in back of the left end, forming two separate divisions (Fig. 2). The right fist, still maintaining its grip, is thrust through the lower section, then back through the upper section, in the direction of the arrow.

This maneuver is extremely simple, due to the flexibility of the rope, which is brought into a crisscrossed formation with the fists still gripping the ends, but with the palms of the hands now upward (Fig. 3). Now, by merely bending the hands inward and downward with a forward tilt, the rope is allowed to slide clear of the hands, which support it, cradle fashion, in what appears to be a large, loose double knot (Fig. 4).

Show this from all angles without pulling on the ends and you will convince people that the knot is genuine; then give the ends a sudden tug and the knot will drop away entirely (Fig. 5). As a variation, you can bring the ends of the rope together and grip them with the right hand only, finishing with a downward shake that dissipates the double knot.

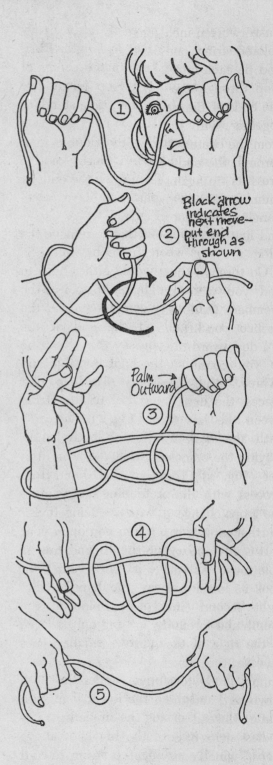

Black arrow indicates next move— put end through as shown

Palm → Outward

LOOP A LOOP

Take two ten-inch lengths of different-colored string, one dark, the other light, and tie each into a loop. Push the dark loop through the light loop and raise the ends of the dark loop so they come together, with the light loop dangling from the center. Put your left forefinger through the ends of the dark loop and press its tip against the tip of your left thumb; then grip the bottom of the dangling light loop between the thumb and first two fingers of your right hand (Fig. 1).

Go through these details a few times and you will find them easy to remember. Exhibiting the loops as described, you lift the light loop and give it a downward tug, repeating the action as you count, "One—two—three!" On "Three," the loops instantly change places, the light loop doubling up between the left thumb and forefinger, with the dark loop dangling below, leaving the onlookers blinking in disbelief (Fig. 2). You repeat the tugging process with the dark loop and again the loops change places in a twinkling. Further repeats can follow.

It is all done with one easy, undetectable move. As you raise the light loop, hook its lower end with the tip of your right second finger; and with your thumb and forefinger, grip either strand at the right of the dark loop (Fig. 3). Release the lower end as the right thumb and forefinger pull sharply downward and the change will be automatic. Instead of strings, you can use endless strips of cotton known as "jersey loops," which come in varied colors and

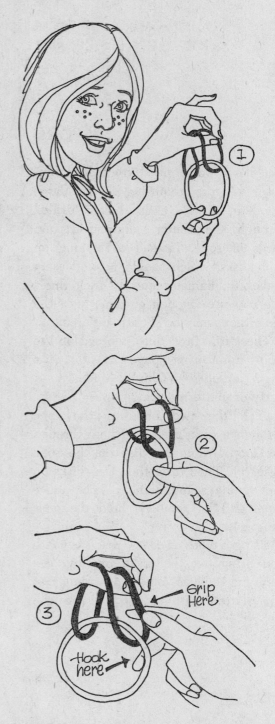

are specially adaptable to this trick because of their flexibility.

27

POKO-CHINKO

This name was applied to a feat of Chinese wizardry requiring several large wooden disks, with holes drilled through the center, along with 1½ yards of rope. Instead of making up such disks, which should be at least 3 inches in diameter and ½ inch thick, you can use wooden curtain rings; the dimensions may be slightly different.

The initial procedure is based on the Coins from String (page 142), but on a larger scale, Poko-Chinko is ideal as a party or platform trick.

Push the two ends of the rope through a disk; then run them through the loop, fixing the disk on the rope (Fig. 1). Then drop the other disks on the double string, tying a knot above them and let someone hold the ends (Fig. 2).

Using a cloth as cover, reach beneath and bring out the disks, one by one, counting them as you go. Assuming that you started with six, stop when you come to five, then pull away the cloth. There, on the rope, firmly tied in place, is the bottom disk, leaving onlookers puzzled as to how you managed to draw the others down over it (Fig. 3). To prove that point, show that it is necessary to untie the knot to remove the disk.

A neat piece of deception at an unsuspected moment produces this bizarre result. You start by looping the first disk on the doubled rope (as in Fig. 1), but when you slide the others on above it, pause when you come to the final disk, in this case No. 6. As you start to slide it on the double rope, spread the ends slightly, so it goes over one end only (Fig. 4).

No one will notice that the sixth ring slides down a single rope, particularly if you follow its downward course with your free left hand while the right hand grips both ends of the rope up above (Fig. 5). With the left hand gripping

both ropes just above the last disk, the
right hand drops the ends and comes
down to join the left hand, so they can
tie a single knot above the disks. By
making the knot loose and inserting a
thumb or finger in the hole, you can
keep the disks well stacked, hiding the
fact that the ropes were separated (Fig.
6).

When you give the ends of the rope
to your helper (as in Fig. 2), tilt them
forward, so the disks will still seem well
stacked when you cover them. From
then on it is truly marvelous, from your
standpoint as well as theirs. Under the
cloth, you release the bottom disk and
the rest come with it—except for the
sixth disk, which is tied to the string.
Since they mistake it for the first disk,
they marvel how it could have happened; while you marvel at how easily
you fooled them!

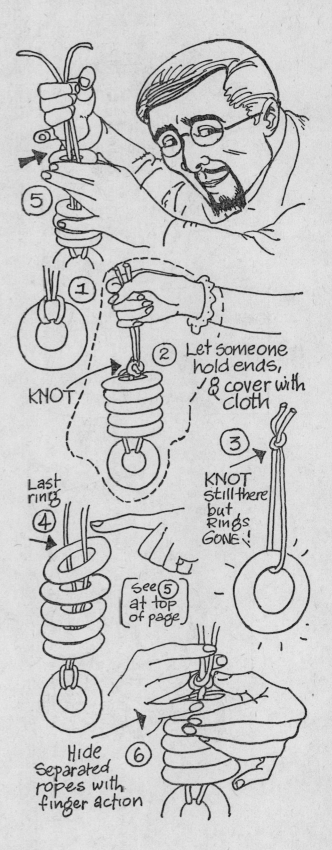

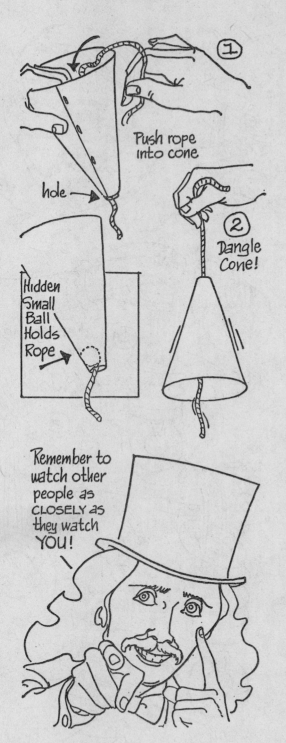

Push rope into cone

hole →

② Dangle Cone!

Hidden Small Ball Holds Rope →

Remember to watch other people as CLOSELY as they watch YOU!

ROPE AND CONE

This is a clever variation of The Bottle Imp using a cone made from fairly stiff cardboard. The cone, which can be stapled, taped, or glued to hold its shape, should have a hole in its tip, like an ice-cream cone, so that a two-foot length of thin rope can be pushed through it. Allow the rope to extend a bit from the cone.

Holding the cone tip downward in your left hand, push the rope down through the cone with your right hand, almost to the end (Fig. 1). Then, gripping the lower end of the rope, let the cone drop, so it dangles point upward, to everyone's amazement (Fig. 2). The secret is a very small ball—either rubber or tinfoil—which you conceal in your right hand while pushing the rope down through the cone. Toward the finish, let the ball drop into the cone and jam the rope as your left hand continues its downward pull.

After the miracle of the suspended cone, grip the cone with your left hand, tilting it to draw the rope downward with the right hand, releasing the little ball so that it drops into your cupped right hand. That enables you to give both cone and rope for examination as the finish of the mystery—except this is not the finish; it is just the beginning.

You can now let other people try it for themselves, to no avail. Have extra cones and rope ready for them, leaving out the ball, of course. Then you can use their cones and ropes to perform the trick—really baffling everyone!

This makes it a wonderful trick for a children's party, where they will all be trying to work it—each having their own cone and rope.

Only don't be too sure of yourself!

There was one magician who did this to what he thought was perfection. He kept showing one child after another just how it should be done, until he had half a dozen all trying it with no success. By then, the first boy who tried it had a great idea. While the magician was showing other children how to fool themselves, this boy simply tied a knot in one end of his rope and pushed the other end through the cone until the knot stopped it. The audience saw him doing this while the magician was busy with the other children.

Then, suddenly, the smart boy said: "Look, Mr. Magician!" And there the boy was dangling the cone from the lower end of the rope, thanks to the hidden knot the magician could not even see, leaving the magician totally nonplused, to the amusement—and *not* the amazement!—of the audience.

So remember this rule: As a magician, be sure to watch other people as closely as they watch you!

TRAVELING KNOTS

Two ropes, each five or six feet in length, are used in this surprising effect, along with two good-sized paper bags. Rope "A" is tied with three single knots in a row (Fig. 1), and the right hand lays these on the *left* so they form a series of coils, each on top of the one before (Fig. 2). The coiled rope (A) is dropped in Bag A, with an end hanging over the edge.

Rope "B" is shown as a simple, plain rope (Fig. 3), and the right hand gathers it into three coils (Fig. 4), placing them on the left hand. They are then dropped into Bag B, with an end protruding, so that the two bags appear (Fig. 5) with the knotted rope on the left, the ordinary rope on the right. All is so fair and above board that the audience will be ready for a big gasp when they see the magical result that follows.

With your left hand, draw Rope A from its bag, showing that the knots have completely vanished; then, with your right hand, bring Rope B from its bag, showing that the knots have arrived there in the interim! (Fig. 6).

It's all done in a smooth, undetectable manner. With Rope A, as the right hand piles the loose knots on the left, the fingers slide the left end of the rope beneath the coils thus formed, and when the rope is dropped into the bag, the right hand draws the left end up through the coils (Fig. 7) and hangs it from the bag. With Rope B, the right hand forms each coil with a reverse twist (as shown in Fig. 4), and the left fingers push the left end up through the coils so the right hand can grip it (Fig. 8) and leave it in sight.

Shake the ropes slightly as you draw them from the bags and the knots will be automatically transposed!

ROPE A ①

ROPE B ③

②

④ Reverse Twist

⑤ BAG A (Knotted rope) BAG B (ordinary rope)

⑥ Knots gone→ Knots appear!

A   B

⑦ Pile up each knot

⑧

GO-GO KNOTS

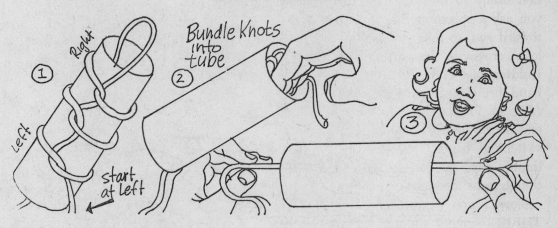

A yard or more of ribbon and a cardboard mailing tube form the needed items for this highly perplexing effect. Starting at the left end of the ribbon, tie the string around the tube with a simple, single knot, leading off to the right. That enables you to tie a second knot in the same fashion and also a third (Fig. 1). You can add even more if the tube and ribbon are long enough, but three is a good number.

Next, tilt the right end of the tube upward and drop the right end of the ribbon down through (Fig. 2). That enables you to draw all the knots upward, bunching them together as you draw them off the end of the tube, thus forming a tight bundle that you push down into the tube itself. That done, you have someone hold the ribbon by the ends, keeping it horizontal as you draw the tube back and forth along the ribbon.

As you do, the onlookers see to their amazement that all the knots have completely vanished! (Fig. 3).

You don't really have to know how the trick is done in order to do it. Just follow the description and it will work itself. Pushing one end down through the tube actually unties the knots in advance, making the finale automatic.

NOTE: This can be worked as a pocket trick with a piece of string and a small, improvised tube; or as a platform presentation with a big tube and a rope so long that two people will be needed to hold the ends!

STRAIGHT THROUGH

One of the fastest tricks on record, this requires a thin rope or tape measuring about three feet in length. The ends are tied firmly to form a strong loop, and you ask a spectator to extend his arm toward you, so that you can stretch the loop crosswise beneath his forearm. Holding one end of the loop in each hand, bring the ends up around his arm (Fig. 1). From there, you thrust the left end of the loop through the right end, switching hands, so that the right thumb grips the left end, and the left thumb grips the right end (Fig. 2).

Now you count "One—two—THREE!" giving a slight tug with the first two counts and a hard yank with the third. As your hands spread wide apart, the entire loop comes straight through the spectator's arm, so fast that he cannot even feel it! (Fig. 3).

It's not only fast, it's also easy. Just after the second tug, hook the outer strand of the rope with your right second finger and release the end with your right thumb as you make the final yank (Fig. 4). The loop whisks around the spectator's arm and comes on top automatically. Practice this around a chair arm or over the back of a chair and you will be all set to dazzle your friends.

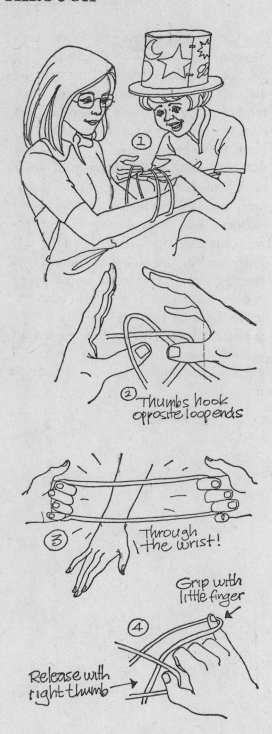

② Thumbs hook opposite loop ends

③ Through the wrist!

④ Grip with little finger

Release with right thumb

35

THE MYSTERIOUS STRING

Tie the ends of a string together, making one continuous loop. Thread a ring on the doubled string, then put the ends of the loop over a person's two forefingers so the string is taut and the ring is on the center of it (Fig. 1). State that you will take the ring away without removing the string from either of the spectator's fingers. And then proceed to do so, leaving only the string.

Here's the trick: Slide the ring toward the forefinger at the left (Fig. 2). Take hold of the string at the right of the ring and draw it into a loop slipping it over the finger at the left. Then remove the loop that was already on the person's finger. This is done in a split second. The string remains taut, still girding both fingers, but the ring drops down free.

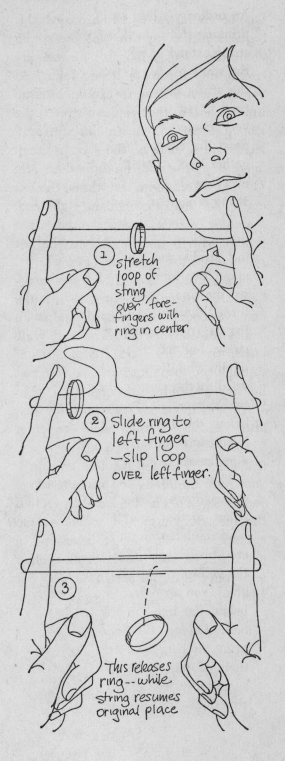

1 stretch loop of string over forefingers with ring in center

2 Slide ring to left finger —slip loop over left finger.

3 This releases ring -- while string resumes original place

STRING AND STRAW

An ordinary string is pushed through a drinking straw, so that both ends of the string extend in full view (Fig. 1). Fold the straw exactly in half, so the ends of the string extend downward, and proceed to cut the string and straw at the very center (Fig. 2). Yet when you press the cut portions of the straw together and draw them straight apart, everyone is amazed to see that the string is completely restored! (Fig. 3).

This mystery depends on a neat bit of preparation. Beforehand, take a drinking straw and cut a lengthwise slit about two inches long near the center. In showing the straw, keep the slit turned downward (Fig. 4). In performing the trick, run the string through the straw, but let the ends protrude unequally while you bend the straw downward at the center. Grip the straw between your left thumb and fingers just below the bend, and with your right hand, draw on the ends of the string to equalize them.

That action brings the center of the string down through the slit in the straw, so that the string is hidden behind the left thumb, which can be lowered further while you keep drawing on the ends of the string (Fig. 5). This enables you to insert a pair of scissors below the bend and cut the straw in half. Laying the scissors aside, you bring the hands together and draw portions of the straw apart, showing the supposedly cut string apparently restored.

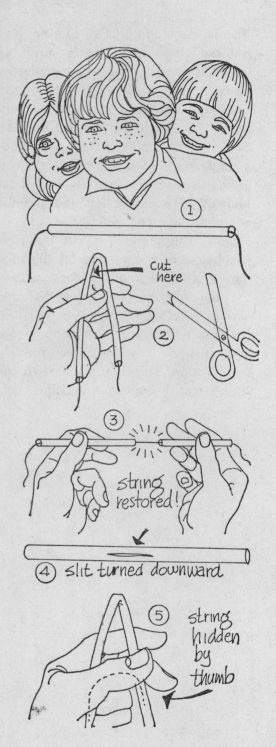

cut here

string restored!

④ slit turned downward

⑤ string hidden by thumb

TRI-CUT ROPE

This is one of the best of the "cut and restored" rope tricks, particularly because it works almost automatically. Using a rope up to six feet in length, bring the right end across to a point midway between the left end and the center of the rope and tie it there with a single knot. Then bring the right end across in the same manner and tie it midway between the left end and the center of the rope.

Now, you pretend to cut the rope just below each knot and let the rope dangle with the knots as markers. Laying the scissors aside, coil the rope around your right hand with your left; then reach into your left coat pocket for some invisible powder that you sprinkle on the rope. The right hand gives the rope a toss, uncoiling it, and the knots

have vanished, leaving the cut rope fully restored!

The secret is this: Instead of cutting the main portion of the rope below the knots, you cut off the tied ends. It looks exactly the same, so no one suspects that you have not actually cut the rope. In winding the rope around your right hand, keep drawing the knots along the rope with your left hand and when you reach into your pocket and pretend to take out some "invisible powder," you leave the knots there. The right hand can then unwind the rope and show it fully "restored," since it was never cut.

NOTE: By putting small marks—preferably with ink—a few inches below each end of the rope, you will know exactly where to cut the rope after you have tied the knots.

CHAPTER FOUR: Dinner-table Magic

T. Nelson Downs

BACK IN THE DAYS of high silk hats, nearly every magician made a practice of plucking coins from the air and dropping them into a "stovepipe," which is what hats were nicknamed. Audiences were fascinated. Today you can have the same results using a hat or a child's sand pail or some similar receptacle. You also need up to a dozen fifty-cent-size coins, which you can keep in your pocket until needed; then bring them out in the bend of your left fingers (Fig. 1 [See page 41 for illustration]).

Keeping the back of your hand toward the audience, grip the pail by the rim so your fingers come inside, where they press the hidden coins against the side of the pail. With your right side toward the audience, show your right hand empty; then make a grab in the air as though catching a coin and dropping it into the pail. Simultaneously, the tips of your left fingers release a coin so that it plunks into the pail (Fig. 2). You then repeat the action, "catching" another coin and "dropping" it into the pail, so you can reach in and bring out both coins, showing them to the spectators.

Now, you actually drop one coin back into the pail and pretend to do the same with the second coin; but instead, you retain it in the bend of your right fingers (Fig. 3). Pointing upward with your forefinger, push the coin upward with your thumb, at the same time bending your forefinger, so the coin comes between the tips of your right thumb and forefinger (Fig. 4). From the audience's view, it looks as though you actually plucked a coin from the air.

Pretending to drop this coin into the pail, draw it into the bend of the right fingers while the left fingers release another coin from their

T. NELSON DOWNS

KING of KOINS

hidden store. Continuing thus, you keep catching coins—always the same coin!—until the supply is exhausted.

The "Aerial Treasury" or "Shower of Money," as it was sometimes called, requires practice in order to time the pretended dropping of the right-hand coin with the release of a coin by the left fingers; but when the knack has been acquired, the trick becomes automatic. A good finish is to dip your right hand into the pail and bring out half a dozen coins or more; then let a few plunk back into the pail, while you retain the rest in the bend of the right fingers. You can then push them up singly with your thumb, dropping each coin openly into the pail after you produce it.

Toward the year 1900, a young man named T. Nelson Downs was busily clicking a telegraph key in Marshalltown, Iowa. When not working, he continuously practiced sleights with coins, inventing new moves and palming methods. He finally gave up his job and went into vaudeville, styling his act the "Miser's Dream." Showing his hat and hands completely empty, Downs spread his fingers wide, so people could see both back and front. He then produced from forty to fifty coins, quite a bit more than the customary dozen.

40

The act was so great that when Downs went to England, he was booked for six solid months at the Palace Theatre in London. As the "King of Koins," he sauntered on the stage with a pleasing, knowing smile, where the glare of the spotlight caught the glint of British half crowns as they materialized from nowhere at the very tips of his deft fingers.

After finishing at the Palace and arranging a return engagement, Tommy—as his friends called him—headed for the Continent. His fame had spread ahead of him; and when he reached Germany, a packed theater was waiting to view his performance. So he was more nonchalant than ever. He smilingly went through the preliminaries, and suddenly his smile faded. All the coins weren't where he needed them. He had left them on his trunk in his dressing room! Downs had to continue, so recalling how old-time magicians made fast grabs

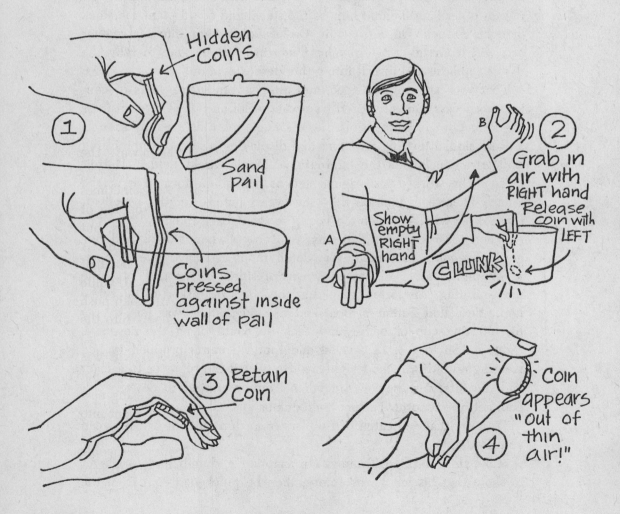

for imaginary coins, Downs did the same, roving the stage, snatching everywhere, and finally bowing off. The audience began to applaud, thinking that the King of Koins must have been too fast for them to see the coins that they assumed he had caught and thrown into the hat. Offstage, Downs grabbed a startled stagehand and tried to explain his dilemma, which was difficult, since Tommy did not speak German and the man knew no English. One word, though, sprang to Tommy's mind, so he kept repeating it: *"Geld—Geld—Geld—"* meaning "money —money—money—" while showing his empty hand and pointing toward his dressing room.

The applause was subsiding, so the King of Koins stepped onstage to take a bow; then he glanced over his shoulder and saw that the stagehand was gone. So Downs roved the stage again, repeating the pantomime of the imaginary coins, this time to dwindling applause. A glance toward the wing told him that the stagehand was back, so he bowed off again, waving the empty hat with one hand and thrusting his other hand behind him, so the stagehand could plant the stack of coins unseen. Onstage again, Downs went right into his regular act, with coins glinting from his fingertips, just in time to rally the dying applause and turn it into a thunderous ovation.

That was back around 1900, and after several more years of continued success, Downs retired from vaudeville and went into business in Marshalltown. He continued to do magic more as a hobby than as a profession, attending functions and displaying his never-diminishing skill. At a conclave of the International Magic Circle, held in Detroit in 1934, he worked his original act, as he had performed it at the Palace Theatre in London thirty-five years before, for the benefit of those of us who had been too young to see it back then.

When I asked about that time in Europe when Downs had forgotten his coins, he recited every detail, much as I have given it here. A few nights later, we elected Downs president of the IMC, and the next morning, a reporter stopped at the hotel and asked to interview him. We called Tommy's room and he said that he was just having his morning cup of coffee, but that we could bring the newsman right up. So four of us arrived and found Tommy propped in bed wearing an old-fashioned nightcap. He waved the reporter to a chair and the interview began. But when Tommy started to describe his coin act, the reporter became incredulous and asked:

"You say that you catch half dollars from thin air. But just how can you do that?"

"Like this," replied Tommy. He snapped a thumb and forefinger to show that his hand was empty; then he plucked a coin from the tip of the reporter's pencil. "And like this"—a snap from the thumb and fingers brought a coin from the reporter's notebook—"and another one up here." Tommy took that one from the bed lamp, so neatly that it seemed to emerge from the lighted bulb. He found another in the mouthpiece of the telephone; then he whisked a handkerchief from the reporter's breast pocket and shook a few more coins from the handkerchief.

Rather than use his nightcap for a hat, Tommy dropped the coins in his empty coffee cup until it was half filled; then he broke open a roll, brought a coin from it, and pushed the coin through the solid side of the cup, where we heard it jingle among the rest.

So the reporter had his story, but he went his way wondering if the editor would believe it. After he had gone, Tommy turned to me and said whimsically:

"After that night in Europe that we talked about, I decided never again to get caught without my coins. Now I even sleep with them."

Next to coins, Downs liked card magic, and although he was skilled in the most difficult sleights, he enjoyed simpler tricks as well. One of his favorites is known as the Piano Trick because it is performed as follows:

Tell a person to place his hands flat on the table, with fingers spread slightly as though about to press the keys of a piano. From a pack of cards, take two cards and rest them, side edge upward, between the last two fingers of the person's right hand, saying, "Two cards—an even number." You then place another pair between the next two fingers, saying, "Two more—still even" and another pair between the next two fingers, saying, "Two more, still even." Another pair goes between the right thumb and forefinger; then a pair between the left thumb and forefinger. Two more go between the first two fingers of the left hand; two more between the second and third fingers of the left hand, in all cases with the comment, "Two more—always even."

That leaves only one available space, between the third and fourth fingers of the left hand. There you set a single card upright, stating, "And here we have just one odd card."

Now, returning to the starting point, lift out the first pair of cards, turn them face down, separate them, and drop them side by side, saying, "Two cards—still even." Do this with the next pair, dropping them separately on the cards already there: "Two more cards—still even." Continue this with each succeeding pair, until you reach the single card. Then you say: "Here we have two piles, *both even.* Which pile do you want?"

Whichever he says, you take the single card and say, "Very well. Here we have one *odd card*. I will place it on your *even pile* to make your pile *odd*." You do that and add: "Now hold your *odd pile* squarely between your hands." As he does that, you pick up the other pile and state: "From this *even pile*, I will send one card into your *odd* pile. That will leave me with an *odd number* and will add a card to your pile, making it even!"

You give your pile a forcible snap and say, "Now let's count the piles and see what happened." Counting your cards, you announce: "One, two, three, four, five, six, seven! Now count yours and you find that you have *eight*." The person does that and finds to his amazement that you are right!

Try this trick yourself and you will find that it actually works itself, which may puzzle you all the more. But a careful study will provide the answer. In separating the pairs into two piles your repeated statement, "Always even" or "Still even" makes people overlook the fact that there are just *seven pairs*, so that each heap is actually *odd* instead of *even*. When thus deluded, the onlookers take all the rest for granted and deceive themselves.

BALANCING THE CUP

Balancing a paper cup on the upraised edge of a paper plate looks very difficult. Actually it is quite easy if the plate is gripped at the edge by the right fingers, which are bent inward and kept toward the spectators. This enables you to extend your right thumb up behind the plate while your left hand is pretending to balance the cup on the upper edge, so the tip of the thumb serves as an added base.

A plastic tumbler can be used instead of a paper cup. But don't risk china plates and cups or a regular drinking glass, as they are too apt to slip and break. If that happens with paper or plastic, you will still have another chance to try the balance.

Presented as a table trick, this effect can prove to be a real surprise. With your left hand, take a playing card—say, the 6 of diamonds—and set it upright while your right hand places a glass on the top edge of the card. When you move your hands away, the card remains upright, with the glass balanced precariously on top of it! (Fig. 1).

A special card is needed for this deception. To prepare it, take an odd card, such as a joker, and bend it in half, lengthwise, so that the halves come back to back. Glue the right half of the joker to the back of the 6 of diamonds from another pack, making sure that the edges come even (Fig. 2).

By pressing the left half flat with the left thumb, this can be shown as an ordinary card. While setting the card upright and placing the glass on top, the left thumb releases pressure and opens the flap toward the right so that it serves as a hidden support for the glass (Fig. 3). After a brief balance, take away the glass with the right hand and the card with the left, closing the flap in the same action so both sides of the card can be shown.

To make the finish more convincing, have the ordinary 6 of diamonds on top of the pack from which you take the specially prepared card. Have the pack laying handy, and at the finish, show the back of the prepared card with the left hand, lay the glass aside with the right, and pick up the pack, placing it face down on the prepared card. As an afterthought, draw off the top card from the pack and put it in the glass,

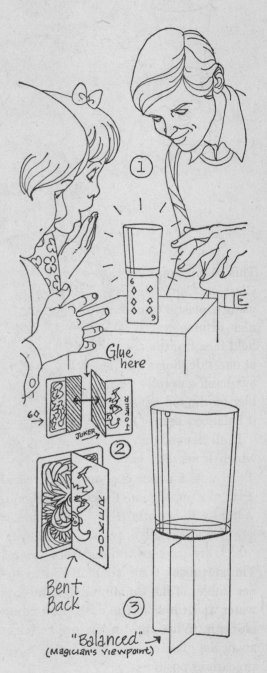

Glue here

② JOKER

③ Bent Back

"Balanced" → (Magician's Viewpoint)

offering both for examination. People seeing the ordinary 6 of diamonds will suppose it to be the card you used for the amazing balance.

AMAZING TUMBLER
BALANCE

This is an impromptu version of the Glass on Card (described on page 46), using a plastic tumbler instead of a regular drinking glass. A playing card is held face front in the right hand, thumb at one side, fingers at the other; and the left hand carefully places a plastic tumbler on the top edge of the card, leaving it balanced there (Fig. 1).

It all depends on the right forefinger, which is secretly extended upward be-hind the card, serving as a hidden prop when the left hand draws the tumbler slightly backward (Fig. 2). Some skill is needed, which makes the balance all the more convincing, especially when the left hand removes the tumbler and passes it for inspection while the right hand offers the card for examination. A paper drinking cup can be used for the balance instead of a plastic tumbler.

BALANCING GLASS

This surprising trick is ideal for the dinner table. Take a half-filled glass of water and tilt it at an angle on the tablecloth. When you move your hands away the glass remains balanced in this precarious position.

Prior to showing the stunt, slip a matchstick beneath the tablecloth. When you proceed to balance the drinking glass choose the spot where the matchstick is located. With the aid of the hidden stick you can balance the glass after a few tries.

CHANGING LIQUIDS

start finish

Plastic
piece in
goblet
to start

Remove Plastic
under Kerchief

Show a small goblet filled with a colored liquid. Cover the glass with a handkerchief. When you remove the cloth, the colored liquid has become water. To prove that this is not a change produced by chemicals, drink the water or ask some other person to do so. The liquid is plain water.

The trick requires a thin, flat piece of transparent colored plastic, cut to fit the glass. This is inserted in a small goblet of water. (Remember: The water must reach the top of the colored plastic—no more, no less.) From the spectators' viewpoint they receive the illusion of a colored liquid. The plastic is carried away with the handkerchief, which you calmly place in your pocket. All that remains is a goblet of water.

THREE-GLASS TURN-UP

This trick is so simple that you can learn it immediately, yet it will prove a baffler to other people when you tell them to try it! Set three glasses in a row, the center glass right side up, the other two upside down (Fig. 1). The trick is to take two glasses, one in each hand, and turn them over; then again take two and turn them over; then repeat the move a third time. At the finish, all three glasses must be right side up (Fig. 2).

Here is the system: Counting the glasses from the left, make the following moves: First, turn over Nos. 1 and 2; second, turn over Nos. 2 and 3; third, turn over Nos. 1 and 2. Being so simple, it would seem that anyone could do it after watching you.

The reason they can't do it is that after you have done it (Figs. 1 to 2), you *turn down* the center glass (Fig. 3) and tell someone to try it. From that position, it won't work in three moves. When *you* repeat the trick, turn *up* the center glass to start (as in Fig. 1). Few people will notice the difference, because they will be too busy watching your moves, hoping to copy them.

FIVE IN A ROW

This is an elaboration of the Three-glass Turn-up in which five glasses are arranged alternately right side up and upside down, the object being to turn over two glasses at a time, bringing them all right side up in just three moves. Starting from Fig. 1 and numbering the glasses from left to right, the following pattern will create the required result:

Move 1: Turn over Nos. 1 and 4.
Move 2: Turn over Nos. 2 and 5.
Move 3: Turn over Nos. 1 and 5.

This brings all five glasses upright (Fig. 2). To repeat the trick, you turn down glass Nos. 2 and 4, putting the row in its original state. When someone else wants to try it, turn up glass Nos. 2 and 4 and then turn the others down (Fig. 3). That makes the feat impossible in three moves, turning two glasses at a time. The use of five glasses makes it easier to fool your audience because the moves are more intricate and there are more glasses to turn down before starting over, making detection less likely.

FIVE MORE IN A ROW

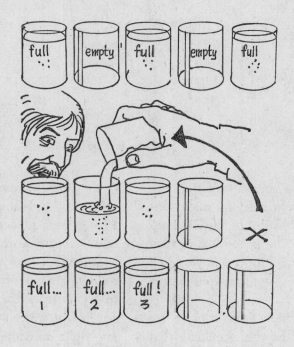

Here is a baffler well suited to the dinner table. You arrange five glasses in a row, running:

FULL EMPTY FULL EMPTY FULL

The trick is to *move just one glass*, yet have three full glasses at one end of the row and two empties at the other.

The more people try it, the more impossible it seems—until—

You pick up the full glass at the right, pour its contents into the second glass from the left, then put it right back at the right! You have moved *just one glass*, yet the trick is done!

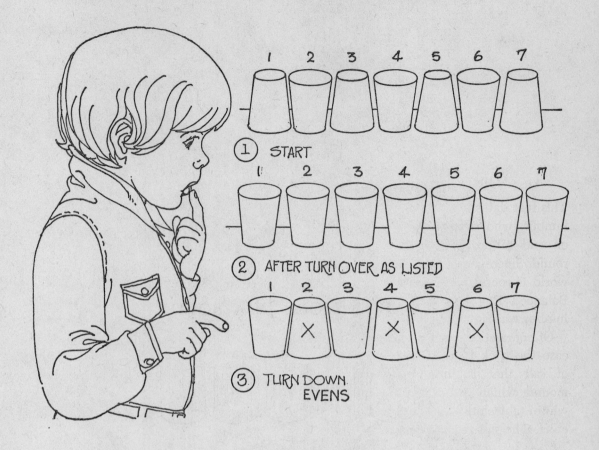

1 START

2 AFTER TURN OVER AS LISTED

3 TURN DOWN EVENS

SEVEN UP

Seven glasses in a row, alternating up-side down and right side up, make this the most advanced form of the Turn-up Glasses (Fig. 1). The purpose is to turn over two glasses at a time, allowing *five* such moves to bring all seven glasses upright (Fig. 2).

However, to make the trick more difficult, it can also be specified that every glass in the row be turned over at least once. To keep track of that, whenever a glass is turned over for the first time, it should be drawn a few inches forward, so the whole line will be that much closer at the finish.

Various moves are possible, but one of the simplest and most effective is the following, counting from left to right: First, 1 and 4; second, 2 and 5; third, 3 and 6; fourth, 4 and 7; fifth, 2 and 6.

Since that many moves are difficult to follow, you can often allow other people to try it from the original setup (Fig. 1), in which the *even*-numbered glasses are right side up to start. But if you want to make sure your audience cannot possibly accomplish the feat, turn *down* those even numbers to start, leaving the odd glasses up, so the row will be set (as in Fig. 3), bringing failure to all who try it.

THE BALANCED EGG

This feat dates back to Christopher Columbus, who supposedly stood an egg on end to prove that the world was round. Since you already know that the world is round, you can duplicate The Balanced Egg just to prove that Columbus was right (Fig. 1).

Of course there is a trick to it; in this case the trick is a fair-sized sprinkling of salt that is formed into a little mound, which will not be noticed on a white tablecloth, napkin, or handkerchief. The salt forms just the right base on which to balance the egg (Fig. 2), although some amount of skill or patience may be needed, which will make it all the more effective. Afterward, you can simply brush the salt away.

If no white cloth is available, the salt can be formed into a mound underneath a tablecloth, napkin, or handkerchief of *any* color. Have it all set beforehand and press the egg down into the cloth just above the mound, which will spread sufficiently to complete the balance.

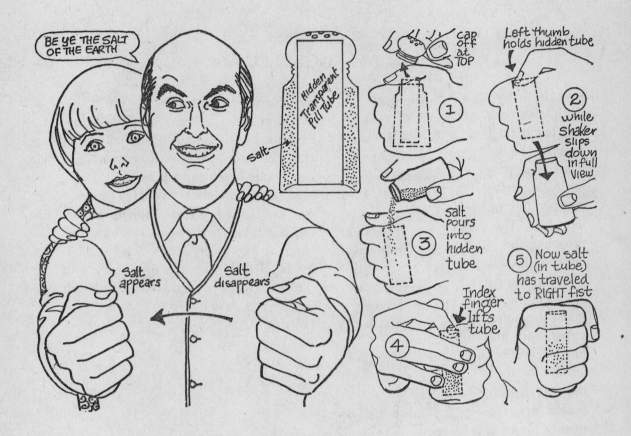

TRAVELING SALT

In this effect, the performer removes the top from an ordinary salt shaker and pours the contents into his left fist. Setting the shaker aside, he extends both arms and closes his right fist. As the left fist squeezes, it is gradually opened to show that the salt is gone. The right fist is then turned downward, and from it you pour the vanished salt!

As an adjunct to this trick, you need a transparent, tube-shaped pill bottle, just narrow enough to fit upright inside a salt shaker, which is partly filled with salt. The tube is then pushed down into the shaker until it is imbedded in the salt, leaving the open end of the tube projecting almost an inch above the mouth of the shaker. The shaker cap is then screwed in place to hide the projecting tip of the tube, and you are set to go.

In performing, pick up the shaker with your left hand, hold it loosely and fairly deeply in your left fist, and turn

54

your left side toward the spectators. With your right hand, unscrew the cap and lay it on the table (Fig. 1). This enables the left thumb to dip downward and press sideways against the projecting tube, the salt shaker being entirely out of sight within the loose left fist. The right hand then approaches the left and grips the shaker between its thumb and fingers, drawing it downward from the left hand.

During this action, the left thumb retains the inner tube by pressing the upper end into the bend of the left fingers, keeping it deep enough in the left fist to remain unseen (Fig. 2). As the left fist tightens around the concealed tube, the right hand casually and openly pours salt from the shaker apparently into the left fist. Actually the salt goes into the tube, until it is almost filled (Fig. 3). The right hand lays the salt shaker on the table beside the cap, then returns to flick away stray grains of salt from the top of the closed left fist.

While doing this, turn your body so that the back of the right hand is toward the spectators. This enables you to bend the right index finger inward and insert it in the opening of the tube (Fig. 4). A tight fit is helpful here, but if the tube is slightly loose, you can still gain a satisfactory grip by pinching the lip of the tube with the tip of middle finger. The right hand is then lifted, with knuckles straight upward, bringing the hidden tube along with it, salt and all (Fig. 5).

The left hand is then raised and extended toward the left, carrying attention in that direction, while the right thumb secretly draws the tube downward from the tip of the index finger, pressing it into the bend of the right fingers so that the right hand can form a fist about the tube, exactly as the left hand did earlier. During this hidden maneuver, the body should be turned frontward, directly toward the spectators, so that the right fist can be extended to the right and both hands will be far apart.

The salt is then "magically" squeezed from the left hand, which is extended palm upward, so that the right fist can just as amazingly pour the salt back into the left hand. The salt can either be dumped on the table or poured back into the shaker by the left hand. Either way, the right hand, still fisted, reaches for the shaker and secretly inserts the tube therein, finally putting the cap on the shaker. Or you can drop the tube in your pocket while reaching for a handkerchief to brush remnants of the salt from your hands.

TURNABOUT KNIFE

Try this for a real surprise when seated at a dinner table. You start by laying a napkin on the table, with two corners pointing away from you, so the napkin is half folded. Next, place a table knife on the napkin, just beyond the center, and call attention to the fact that the blade of the knife is toward the right (Fig. 1).

Working with both hands, you roll the doubled center around the knife until you reach the far end; then you simply unroll it toward you (Fig. 2). When you finish unrolling it, the knife naturally comes into sight again, but for some mysterious reason, the knife has turned completely about, with its blade now pointing to the left! (Fig. 3).

It all depends on a look-alike knife, which is concealed between the double fold at the center of the napkin, with its blade pointing the other way. Have the napkin in your lap and lay it carelessly on the table, smoothing it out to form a triangle pointing away from you, with the upper corner more advanced. Lay the first knife on the double fold and roll the two knives forward together.

The under corner will automatically flip over first (Fig. 4). The moment it does, you reverse the action and unroll the napkin toward you. The upper corner has become the lower, so the hidden knife comes out on top. Lift the knife with one hand, and with your other hand, slide the napkin into your lap, taking the original knife with it.

NOTE: The flatter the knives, the better, as there will be less bulge in the napkin.

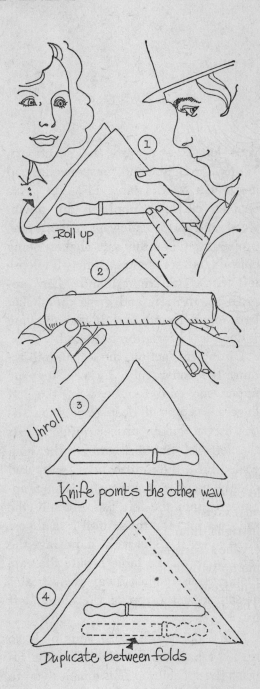

1 Roll up

2

3 Unroll — Knife points the other way

4 Duplicate between folds

56

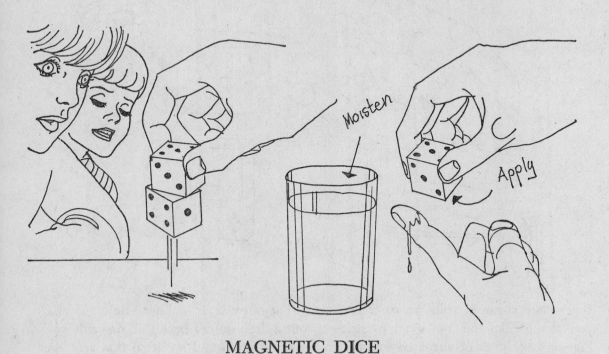

MAGNETIC DICE

Take a pair of dice and set one "five" side on the other so that the spots conform exactly. Lift the upper die with your right thumb and forefinger, and to everyone's surprise the lower die will come up with it, just as if the dice were magnetized!

That is, to everyone's surprise except your own. Just prior to this demonstration of pretended magnetism, you secretly moistened the tip of your left second finger. In picking up the upper die, casually slide its five side along your left fingertip. The moisture thus obtained will cause the dice to adhere.

MAGIC SUGAR LUMPS

If you like sugar in your tea or coffee, you should like this quick table trick. Placing one lump of sugar on another, you lift the upper lump, and the lower lump comes up with it (Fig. 1). Showing the clinging lumps from all angles, you drop them in your coffee and let people wonder whether the sugar lumps were magnetized or whether they were personally mesmerized.

The answer is neither. Beforehand, put a little dab of butter on one side of a sugar lump and lay it so that side is toward you. Press that side downward on the lower lump and the trick will practically work itself (Fig. 2). Dropping the magnetic lumps into a cup of tea or coffee will dispose of the evidence.

STAND-UP MATCHPACK

Here is a very clever table trick with an ordinary matchpack. You open the pack, showing it full of matches (Fig. 1), then close it and balance it upright on the table (Fig. 2). Afterward, you open it again and show the matches as you did before.

Now for the secret: In opening the pack, bend a match downward with your right thumb, which keeps it hidden while you show the matches (Fig. 3). Close the pack and use the bent match as a prop on the side away from the audience's view (Fig. 4), thus balancing the pack on the table (as shown in Fig. 2). Pick up the pack and reopen it, reversing the process to push the match back where it belongs.

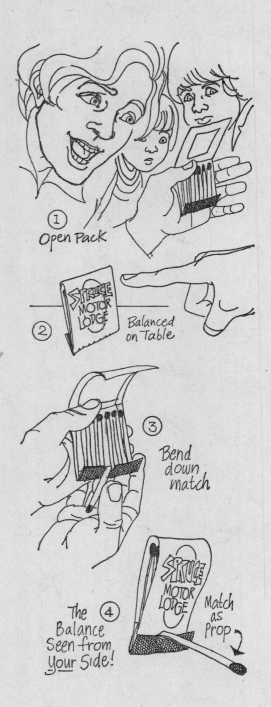

① Open Pack

② Balanced on Table

③ Bend down match

④ The Balance Seen from your Side!

STRUGE MOTOR LODGE

Match as Prop

JUMPING CHOPSTICK

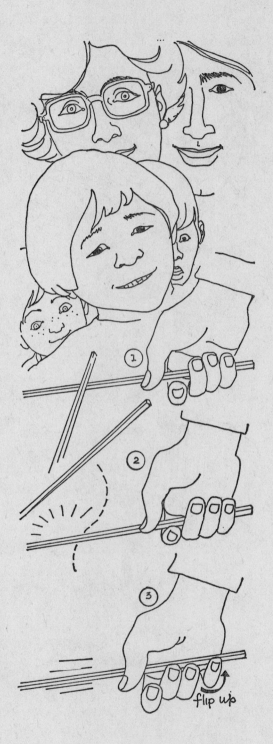

flip up

This is a quick but puzzling trick, using a pair of Chinese chopsticks, that will dazzle any youngster. Hold one at its near end, between the tips of right thumb and first three fingers, just above table level, so that the left hand can slant the other chopstick across it, at the far end (Fig. 1). A magic wave of the left hand and the leaning chopstick does a flying leap and turnover of its own accord (Fig. 2).

The secret is a sharp upward snap of the right third fingertip against the inner end of the chopstick (Fig. 3). Though short and almost too slight to notice, this provides the needed power to put the leaning chopstick into flight, with the wave of the left hand hiding the right finger's action. Drinking straws can be used for this effect if chopsticks are not available.

AROUND THE TABLE

Using common objects from the dinner table, lay them in a circle and tell a person to mentally choose one. Then have him turn away, so that you can start tapping objects, saying, "Go!" with each tap. He is to spell the name of the chosen object mentally, a letter for each tap, and say "Stop!" when he reaches the final letter.

He does this, and when he turns around after saying "Stop!" he is amazed to find you pointing directly to the chosen object, with all the onlookers agreeing that you picked it without hesitation.

It all depends on the objects used for the test. Pick those that spell with a different number of letters; for example,

C-U-P=3; F-O-R-K=4; K-N-I-F-E=5; S-A-U-C-E-R=6; and P-I-T-C-H-E-R= 7. Tap any objects for the first two; then tap the CUP for No. 3; the FORK for No. 4; and so on. This automatically completes the spelling on the chosen object.

Other items may be used as alternates, such as SPOON or GLASS for No. 5; NAPKIN for No. 6; MUSTARD or KETCHUP for No. 8. The number of items can also be increased by adding items with longer names that happen to be available, such as: MACARONI or MAGAZINE for No. 8; SPAGHETTI or CIGARETTE for No. 9; and WATER-MELON for No. 10.

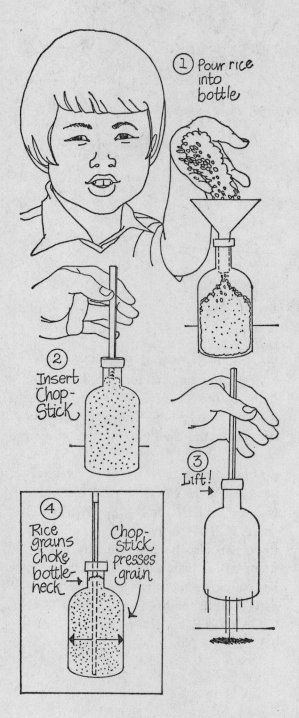

① Pour rice into bottle

② Insert Chop-stick

③ Lift!

④ Rice grains choke bottle-neck   Chop-stick presses grain

A CHINESE MYSTERY

You start this by filling a small, narrow-necked bottle with rice, using a funnel or cone-shaped drinking cup to pour the rice (Fig. 1). Taking a simple wooden chopstick, you push it down into the bottle of rice (Fig. 2), pronounce a few Chinese incantations, and raise the chopstick straight upward. To every-one's amazement, the bottle of rice comes up with it (Fig. 3). Yet all can be examined later.

Surprisingly, this trick works itself. Pushing the chopstick well down into the rice packs the grains so tightly that they actually grip the chopstick so firmly that it can lift the bottle (Fig. 4). To release it, hold the bottle tightly with one hand and twist the chopstick with the other as you draw it out. The trick can be worked with a strong drinking straw, swizzle stick, or pencil.

CHAPTER FIVE: Bafflers
and Participation Tricks

Harry Houdini

THE TRICK THAT BAFFLED HOUDINI

WHEN HARRY HOUDINI was appearing as a headliner on the Keith Vaudeville Circuit in 1922, he went backstage at another theater to talk to Emil Jarrow, a comedy magician who specialized in clever tricks with cards and objects borrowed from the audience. The stage doorman, who wore a rather frayed and faded uniform, recognized Houdini and ushered him to Jarrow's dressing room, where the two magicians were soon talking business.

Houdini was conducting a campaign against fake mediums who claimed they could get messages from "spirits" and cause objects to materialize or dematerialize while "sitters" were grouped around a table. What Houdini wanted was a trick that would match the claims of the fakers, yet afterward could be explained to people in such simple form that they would realize how completely they had been duped.

"Small magic is your specialty," Houdini told Jarrow, "so I felt that you could come up with something that will fill the bill. If you can, you can name your price for it. But it has to be both clever and easy."

Jarrow pondered; then nodded. "I've got it, Harry," he said, "but we'll need a few more people for an audience. The other acts have gone out for lunch, but I'll see if any are still around."

None happened to be around, so Jarrow brought in the doorman as a witness. Jarrow rolled up his sleeves, picked up a watch that was lying on the dressing-room table, and held it in his right hand, which

he covered with a handkerchief. Turning his hand downward, he invited Houdini to reach up from beneath and make sure the watch was still there. Houdini did and agreed that it was. Jarrow told the doorman to do the same, and as soon as the doorman gave a nod, Jarrow said to Houdini, "Grip my right arm, below the sleeve, so there's no chance of any trickery."

Houdini not only gripped the arm that Jarrow thrust in his direction, he also watched it closely, as did the doorman. With his left hand, Jarrow suddenly whisked away the handkerchief and turned his right hand upward—empty! The watch was gone, dematerialized, unless there was a trick to it; and the only way to prove there wasn't, was to bring it back. So Jarrow turned his right hand downward, covered it again with the handkerchief, and had both Houdini and the doorman reach up beneath and assure themselves that his hand was empty. Another whisk of the handkerchief and there was the watch, back again in Jarrow's upturned hand!

With that, Houdini suggested that he and Jarrow go out to lunch. Over the coffee cups, Houdini asked Jarrow how much he wanted for the trick.

"From you, nothing," said Jarrow. "Maybe it looked better than it really is. I'd want you to be satisfied, Harry."

"I told you that if I liked it, you could name your price," reminded Houdini. "That offer still stands."

Again, Jarrow pondered. Then: "I'll make a proposition," he said. "Remember that beaten-down uniform that the doorman is wearing? He wants a new jacket for it, but the theater won't give him the money. Suppose I tell him to go and buy one and send the bill to you."

Houdini gave Jarrow a steady, somewhat quizzical look; then, with just a slight trace of a knowing smile, he said:

"It's a deal."

In May 1923, Houdini told a group of New York magicians that he could duplicate a medium's feat known as an "apport," whereby a solid object is transported from one place to another and back again. He borrowed a half dollar, had someone note its date, and called upon a wealthy skeptic named Joseph Rinn to mark the coin with a pencil so he could identify it later. Houdini then laid the coin on his outstretched right palm, covered it with a handkerchief, and told members of the group to feel the coin beneath the cloth.

Rinn, who had offered ten thousand dollars to any medium who could produce a genuine apport, was so interested in the test that he insisted upon feeling the coin like all the rest. Yet when Houdini lifted the handkerchief, the borrowed coin was gone. Houdini pointed to a hat lying on a table at the opposite side of the room and told Rinn he would find the coin there. Rinn went to the table, dipped his hand in the hat, and not only brought out the coin, but also identified the mark that he had made on it.

While the group of magicians blinked in amazement, Houdini told Rinn to drop the coin back in the hat. With his coat off and his right shirt sleeve rolled high above his elbow, Houdini again covered his right hand with the handkerchief and let everyone feel his empty palm, to make sure there was nothing there. As a convincer, Houdini insisted that Rinn, the complete skeptic, make the final checkup, since he was ready to wager ten thousand dollars that the coin could not possibly come back.

But it did come back. When Houdini lifted the handkerchief, there it was, the borrowed coin, exactly as Rinn had marked it. That put Houdini in something of a dilemma. Either he had to admit it was a trick by explaining it to the magicians, or he had to demand that Rinn hand over a certified check for ten thousand dollars, which he said he would be ready to deliver to anybody who could prove that the impossible had been accomplished. So Houdini explained the trick to his fellow magicians.

It all went back to that day with Jarrow, when Houdini specified the type of trick he wanted. Jarrow had come up with a bold but clever idea. He had called in the stage doorman as an innocent by-stander to witness the trick; but the doorman—to his own amazement—had turned out to be less innocent than he looked. When Jarrow had asked him to feel the watch and make sure it was still there, Jarrow had forcefully planted it in the doorman's hand, even closing the doorman's fingers over it. Then, thrusting his arm toward Houdini, he had called attention to his sleeve, drawing it still farther up, to prove there could be no chance of trickery. Naturally, Houdini went along with that, since Jarrow was known to be an expert when "sleeving" was involved.

In short, the trick was really over when Houdini thought it was just about to begin, so it was not surprising that his attention was drawn from the real source of the mystery. So Jarrow boldly reversed the process to bring the watch back, insisting that the doorman feel his empty hand beneath the handkerchief, giving Jarrow his chance to take back the watch that the doorman still held.

Jarrow practically gave away the secret when he suggested that Houdini buy the doorman a new jacket in return for it, which Houdini promptly did. But the trick was well worth the price—and more—for after Houdini went over the details with Jarrow, he was able to build it into the type of mystery he wanted. Where Jarrow liked to concentrate on an individual spectator, such as Houdini, using a chance by-stander like the doorman as a stooge, Houdini specialized in committee work, so if he needed a helper, he picked the most important man in the group, as in the case of Rinn.

Either course is excellent, but the techniques differ. With Jarrow's method, you keep your palm turned downward, so you can place the object squarely in your helper's hand, nudging it aside, so you can swing your own hand in the opposite direction. This enables you to get away with an object like a watch or small ball, later regaining it as described. With Houdini's method, you use a flat object, preferably a borrowed coin, keeping your palm turned upward so that your helper, somewhat skilled in his own right, can "steal" the object from beneath the handkerchief and replace it in the same way.

With Rinn, Houdini amplified the routine by having him look in a hat, find the coin, and apparently leave it there after letting other people inspect it. Since all that was pretense on Rinn's part, he was actually doing the trick instead of Houdini, which made it all the more baffling. Having put it to the test, Houdini was eager to have fellow magicians perform the trick, because whenever they worked it, they were proving that they could match the claims of pretended mediums, so during the next few years, it gained widespread popularity throughout the world of magic.

It was during that period that I first saw the trick, but even then, its origin had been almost completely forgotten. Houdini had not mentioned Jarrow when presenting it as a "spirit test," and the few magicians who saw Houdini perform it had shown it to others, who in turn had passed it along to still more, so that tracing it back was almost impossible. Nearly twenty-five years later, the trick itself had practically faded into oblivion when I became editor of *The Conjurors' Magazine* and arranged with Jarrow to run some of his long-cherished secrets.

During our discussions, Jarrow told me the story of Houdini and the doorman, but I did not have a chance to use it before *Conjurors'* suspended publication in 1949. Still, I had no idea how the trick had gotten into circulation until Joseph Rinn sent me a copy of his memoirs, which appeared in 1950 and contained a full account of the magicians' meeting where Houdini had baffled the group with the trick that had baffled him when Jarrow performed it a year earlier.

Nearly thirty more years have passed since I pieced together this story involving three long-remembered names in magic—Jarrow, Houdini, and Rinn—so here it is and the trick along with it. Try it and if you pick the right person to help you, chances are that people who witness it will find it as baffling as ever!

TICK-TACK-TOE

Most people are familiar with the game "Tick-Tack-Toe" where two players take turns marking X's and O's in squares until one wins by lining up three-of-a-kind in a row. Here is a magical form of the game that will baffle your friends whenever you perform it.

From a sheet of thin paper, cut a square measuring exactly eight inches by eight inches. Using a pencil and ruler, divide the paper into two-inch squares. Then, with a heavy marker, insert an X and an O in alternate arrangement, filling the squares as follows:

```
X   O   X   O
O   X   O   X
X   O   X   O
O   X   O   X
```

Show the marked sheet and fold the upper portion downward and front-ward, forming a crease through the center of the second cross-row from the top (Fig. 1). Fold the lower portion backward and upward, forming a crease through the center of the second cross-row from the bottom (Fig. 2).

Now fold the right edge frontward, over to the left, creasing the center of the second row from the right (Fig. 3). Then fold the left edge backward to the right, creasing the second row from the left (Fig. 4). This gives you a perfect square, which you fold closed diagonally (Fig. 5) to form a triangle, which you then fold in half to form a smaller triangle (Fig. 6).

Turn that triangle around bringing its short point upward. Hold the triangle in one hand and with a good stout pair of scissors in your other hand you say:

"Tick-tack-toe—all in a row—

Which do you want? An X or an O?"

Whichever the spectator says, you clip the triangle straight upward from base to apex (Fig. 7). Whichever is chosen—"X" or "O"—clip a trifle toward that side (you should be able to see an "X" or an "O" through the paper) and all the chosen squares, in this case the O's, will come out individually, so you can give them to the chooser while you spread out the others, still joined together (Fig. 8).

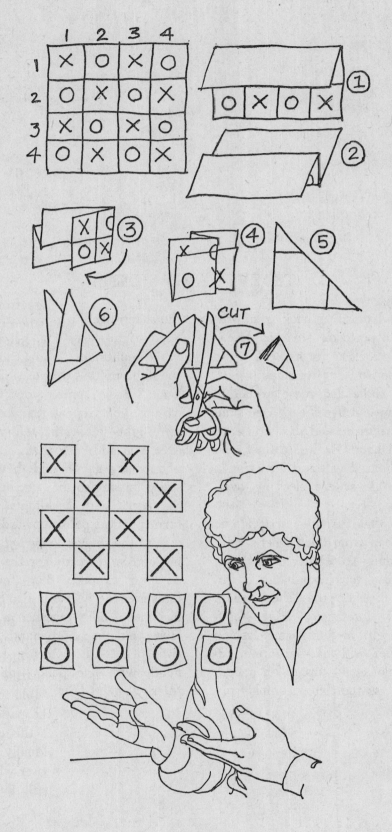

THIEVES AND SHEEP

This fast and puzzling trick is surprisingly easy to perform. This has practically become a classic in its field. Use a sheet of paper to form five small pellets, alike in size and shape; these are laid in a row to represent five sheep. Two similar pellets are made and shown in each outstretched hand. Each is a thief, and the hands themselves stand for barns in which the thieves are sleeping overnight (Fig. 1).

You state that the thieves decide to steal the sheep from the farmer's yard, one at a time. To illustrate this, you close your fists, turn your hands downward, and pick up the "sheep" with thumb and forefinger: Right—left—right—left—right in alternating fashion (Fig. 2). Then add that the farmer became suspicious and turned on a light in his house, so the thieves quickly put the sheep back in the yard: Left—right—left—right—left (Fig. 3).

You continue: "The farmer put out the light and the thieves stole the sheep again." Still keeping your fists loosely closed, you repeat the earlier pickup: Right—left—right—left—right. However, you add: "Meanwhile, the farmer phoned the sheriff and they found the sheep missing so they decided to search the barns with flashlights." Here you turn your fists palms upward and state:

"But the thieves knew what was coming and were ready for them. So what do you suppose they found? Both thieves sound asleep in one barn and all five sheep safely together in the other!" Here you open both hands and reveal two pellets—the thieves—in the left hand; with five pellets—the sheep—in the right hand (Fig. 4).

What makes this trick smooth and effective is the fact that it really works itself. Follow the routine exactly as given and you will see why. Most people overlook the fact that you are using an odd number of pellets—five—to represent the sheep, so when you pick them up alternately, beginning with the right, your right hand will have three sheep and your left hand only two. Adding each thief, that gives the right hand *four* pellets; the left hand, *three*.

In replacing five pellets on the table, you start with the *left hand,* which therefore lays down *three* supposed "sheep" while the *right hand* lays down only *two*. This leaves the left hand empty while the right hand retains two pellets. The final pick-up, right—left—right—left—right, therefore, gives you five "sheep" in the barn on the right and two "thieves" in the barn on the left, and the miracle is accomplished.

② Pick up RIGHT - LEFT - RIGHT - etc .
③ Put back LEFT - RIGHT - LEFT - etc ....

SURPRISE!
④

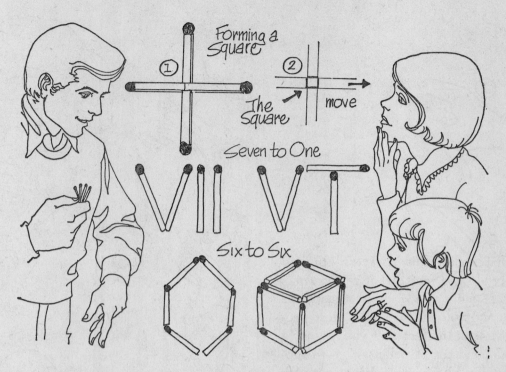

THREE MATCHSTICK BAFFLERS

The three puzzling propositions that follow are all of a sophisticated type, requiring some knowledge of mathematics or geometric figures toward their solution.

FORMING A SQUARE Here you begin by forming a cross with four matches, arranging them exactly as shown in Fig. 1. You then challenge anybody to move *one match only*, yet make the matches form the sides of a perfect square. Seemingly impossible, unless you know the answer!

The secret is to move the match at the right a trifle outward, leaving a tiny square formed by the *bases* of the matches (Fig. 2). This meets the specified conditions, which did not mention the size of the proposed square.

SEVEN TO ONE Five matches are arranged to form the letters VII, which most people recognize as the Roman numeral for 7 (Fig. 1). By moving just one match, it can be changed into the equivalent of the number 1. You claim you can do it, and when people give up, you can show them how.

Here's how: Move the match on the right to a horizontal position stemming from the letter V (Fig. 2). Mathematicians will recognize that as the symbol for the "square root of one." Since that happens to be +1 or −1, you have made it the equivalent of 1.

SIX TO SIX Six matches are arranged to form a hexagon, the geometric term for a six-sided figure (Fig. 1). The proposition is to add three more matches and thus form another six-sided figure.

This is done by inserting the three matches (as shown in Fig. 2). Study it in perspective and you will see that it represents a cube, another six-sided geometric figure!

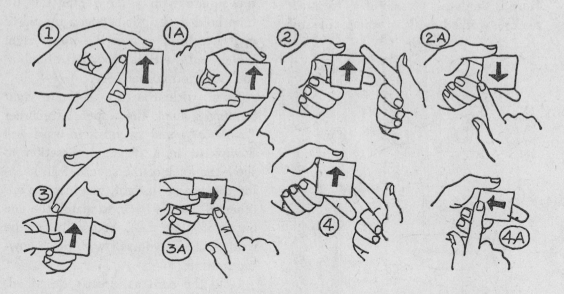

For this baffler, you need a small square of cardboard, on which you draw an arrow, pointing straight upward. Hold the square in your left hand, with your forefinger pressing the corner at the upper right and your thumb pressing the corner at the lower left. With your right finger, hook the upper left corner and swivel the card downward and forward to the lower right, bringing the other side to view. Mark another upward arrow on that side.

Now, every time you hold the card and turn it downward as described, the arrow will point upward on both sides (Figs. 1 and 1A). To make the arrow act in a magical manner, take the square with your right hand and shift your left thumb to the upper left corner and your left forefinger to the lower right. This enables the right forefinger to swivel the square downward and for-

ward from upper right to lower left, which causes the arrow to point down (Figs. 2 and 2A). Keep repeating this and, with each turnover, the arrow will point up—down—up—down, much to everyone's surprise.

If you hold the arrow upright, with your left thumb at the left side and your left forefinger at the right, a simple downturn by the right forefinger will make the arrow point to the right (Figs. 3 and 3A), only to point upward when the square is given another downturn. In contrast, you can point the arrow upward and hold the square with your left thumb at the top and your left forefinger at the bottom. With your right forefinger, swivel the card forward and to the left, which will make the arrow point to the left (Figs. 4 and 4A).

TOPSY-TURVY NUMBERS

Here is the latest version of a "turnover teaser" worked with a square of stiff

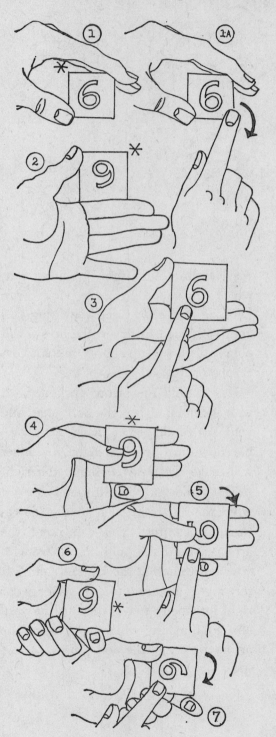

cardboard measuring from 1½ to 2 inches each way. Inscribe the front of the square with a large numeral "6"; then hold it upright between the tip of your left forefinger at the upper right corner and the tip of your left thumb at the lower left corner (Fig. 1).

Now, with the tip of your right forefinger, hook the upper left corner (marked *) and swivel it forward and downward in a diagonal direction to show the back of the square. Still keeping the square upright, you inscribe another "6" on the back, to match the one on front (Fig. 1A). You will then be ready to baffle yourself with the following routine:

Hold the card as already described, showing either side with the "6" straight upward. Do the diagonal down-turn with the right forefinger, showing an upright "6" on the other side and repeat it several times, commenting: "A '6' on each side—always a '6.'" Then take the square in your right hand, keeping the same side constantly in view, and invert the square, saying, "When we turn it upside down, it becomes '9.'"

Meanwhile, you turn your left hand palm frontward, so that when you replace the square with the "9" upright between the left thumb and forefinger, the thumb presses the upper left corner, and the forefinger engages the lower right corner. No one is apt to note the difference, for since the number is still upright, people will be thinking in terms of top and bottom, where the square is concerned (Fig. 2). But when your right forefinger turns over the square forward and downward from the upper right corner (*), it follows a new diagonal, and the square now shows a "6" (Fig. 3).

Remarking that the "9" is topheavy, you again invert the square with your right hand, replacing it between left thumb at upper left and left forefinger at lower right. Another diagonal turnover from upper right downward and the "9" again becomes a "6." After a few repeats, you switch to another system, namely:

Place the square with the "9" upward between the left thumb at the left edge and the left forefinger at the right edge (Fig. 4). With the right forefinger, bring the top edge downward and forward, turning the square over. This time the "9" plops sideways, practically on its back (Fig. 5). Set the "9" upright (as in Fig. 4) and repeat the action (as in Figs. 4 and 5).

Now, for variety, set the square "9" upward with the left thumb pressing the top edge and the left forefinger at the bottom. This enables the right forefinger to swivel the right edge forward and to the left (Fig. 6). Again, the "9" goes sideways, this time plopping "face down" (Fig. 7). That gives you another idea. The right hand holds the square in that exact position so the left hand can shift its thumb to the left side and its forefinger to the right side. From there, the right forefinger brings the top edge downward and forward, finishing the turnover with a "6."

That gives you a better idea. By reversing the moves, you bring the "6" back up to "9." The right thumb swivels the bottom edge of the square upward and backward. The left thumb and forefinger shift from the side edges to the top and bottom (Fig. 7). The right

thumb then swivels the square frontward to the right so the "9" reappears (Fig. 6).

You then remark that since turning the card downward always produced a "6," turning it upward should always produce a "9." To prove it, set the card "6" upward with left thumb at upper left corner and left forefinger at lower right corner (as in Fig. 3). With your right thumb, swivel the lower left corner upward and forward, so the diagonal turnover shows a "9" on the other side (as in Fig. 2).

Immediately take the square in your right hand so the left can do a forward turn and press its forefinger against the upper right corner while its thumb presses the lower left corner. Now, with the right forefinger, hook the lower right corner and swivel it upward and forward along the diagonal. This turnover will bring the other "9" to view (as in Fig. 1), and you can repeat the procedure as often as you wish.

This routine has been described *from your viewpoint,* as that is both the easiest way to learn it and to appreciate its surprising effects. In demonstrating it to other people, it is best to turn your right side toward the onlookers and extend your left hand far enough to view proceedings while the others are looking on so you can enjoy it too!

Emphasize the fact that turning the square *downward* always brings a "6," while turning it upward will result in a "9." Emphasize it as a "fact" because it has no bearing on the case. That helps to puzzle people all the more. Add any variations of your own as you go along. They help to make the trick more fun.

MAGIC SEVEN

Whether you term this an experiment in "thought coincidence" or a process of "mental elimination," it will work perfectly every time you try it, provided you follow the simple procedure exactly as described. All you need are seven playing cards placed in a face-down row and a single coin to go with them. Drop the coin on a card and state that while your back is turned, you want someone to move the coin to the next card in the row, in either direction, every time you give the word, "Move."

You can demonstrate this with some sample moves, showing how the coin might simply be moved back and forth, or moved progressively to the end of the line, according to choice. Since you have no control over the moves, it might wind up anywhere without your knowledge. However, you will try to picture its position mentally, and at intervals you will call upon the person to take away a card from the row before making further moves. Your purpose is to eliminate all the cards until only one remains, sight unseen, with the coin resting on that final card.

To do this, you will obviously have to visualize the coin's exact position during certain stages of the process, as any mistake can mean failure. Except that you not only don't intend to fail, you won't! Here is the reason why:

Since there are seven cards, mentally number them 1 to 7, from left to right. To start the action, drop the coin on any odd card—1, 3, 5, or 7. You can mention that you must see the starting point so that you can follow the spectator's moves mentally. Proceed this way:

Starting with seven cards, give the word "Move" just seven times; then you say, "Now take away the card at the left end of the row."

Now having six cards, you say "Move" six times; then you say, "Take away the card at the right end of the row."

With the five cards remaining, you say "Move" five times; and add, "Take away the card at the left end of the row."

Down to four cards, you give the order "Move" four times and tell the person, "Take away the card at the right."

With three cards, you call for three "moves" of the coin and say, "Take away the card at the left end."

With two cards, you say "Move" twice and order the person, "Take away the card at the right end."

That automatically narrows it down to the lone card now covered by the coin.

NOTE: If a finicky spectator wants to start by placing the coin on a card of his own choice, you can allow him that privilege, provided you watch where he puts it. If he lays it on a card at an odd position (1, 3, 5, 7), proceed as usual; but if he puts it on an even card (2, 4, 6), you count that *as his first move,* and simply order six more to make your regular total of seven.

THE BENDING PENCIL

Borrow a pencil and hold it by one end between your right thumb and forefinger. Tell your audience to watch the pencil intently while you move it up and down. The pencil seems to lose its shape and bend like rubber, yet it is a real pencil.

It all depends on a remarkable illusion achieved by the motion of the pencil. Hold it horizontally and wiggle it with short, quick shakes, which will make it appear to bend.

TRICK OF THE MONTH

Several monthly sheets torn from last year's calendar are the items used in this mystery. These are laid on the table and a spectator chooses one, keeping his choice to himself. The sheets are then mixed and turned over, bringing the blank sides up. You tell the chooser to spell his month letter by letter as you tap the sheets at random and to say "Stop!" on the final letter; and when you turn up that sheet it proves to be his month.

It all depends on the months you use. The layout shows MAY, JUNE, APRIL, AUGUST, OCTOBER, NOVEMBER, SEPTEMBER, each with one more letter than the month preceding it, ranging from three letters up to nine. Instead of mixing the months as you turn them down, you actually lay them in a special order, as:

	APRIL	MAY
AUGUST	JUNE	SEPTEMBER
OCTOBER		NOVEMBER

Make your first two taps on any months; then tap them in numerical order, following a zigzag pattern:

```
      5       3
   6      4      9
      7       8
```

Whatever the month, you will turn it up when the chooser says "Stop!" as you tap the final letter. In repeating the trick, substitute extra months for some that you originally used, as JULY for JUNE, MARCH for APRIL, JANUARY for OCTOBER, DECEMBER for NOVEMBER. Others (MAY, AUGUST, SEPTEMBER) must remain the same.

THE MYSTIC WATCH

While you are out of the room, a watch is set at any desired hour, and then placed face down on the table. When you return you look at the back of the watch, without touching it, and name the hour indicated by the hands.

A confederate from among the spectators is required for this baffler. This person is the one who places the watch on the table. He and you have previously agreed to consider one side of the table as the "top edge." When he places the watch, the confederate sets it so that the stem points toward the desired number of an imaginary circle, the "top edge" of the table representing 12. By glancing at the watch you know the hour at which the hands have been set.

AMAZING MATCH BALANCE

Balancing a wooden match upright on the tip of your forefinger is really amazing, particularly when other people try it and just can't make the match stand up. They can't because there is a secret to the trick that nobody is apt to guess. Beforehand, break off a tiny tip from the lower end of the match. In starting the balance, press the match firmly downward with your thumb; this imbeds the frayed end in the flesh of the forefinger so the match stays upright when the thumb is lifted. It won't work when others try it with ordinary matches.

SNAP!

Extend your right hand and with your left hand place a wooden match across the middle finger of your right, pressing the ends of the match with the first and third fingers. Have other people do the same; then raise your right hand and bring it down, counting, "1—2—Snap!" When you do it, the match breaks in half; with anyone else, the match remains intact.

Naturally, there is a trick to it. After showing everyone else just how to place their matches, remove yours momentarily, and in replacing it, raise your right middle finger and slide the match *below* it, resting the ends of the match on the other two fingers. Start your up-and-down count before anyone notes the difference. Your match will snap as downward pressure provides the finger with added power.

SMASH!

Rest the cover of a matchbox on one of its narrow sides; and on the upper side, place the drawer of the box so that it stands crosswise on one end, a very easy balance. Now challenge anyone to clench a fist and smash the box and cover with a hard downward stroke. This looks easy, too, but the harder the blow, the farther away the box and the drawer will fly!

Steps
1-2-3
Same as
DROP AWAY
KNOT

④

KNOT ⑤

DO AS I DO CARD TRICK

Two packs of cards are required for this trick. You shuffle one and a spectator shuffles the other; then exchange packs and shuffle them again. After a few more exchanges, tell the spectator, "Do as I do." With that, cut your pack in three face-down piles, and he does the same with his pack. Then each of you peek at and return the card on top of the middle heap of your own pack. After that drop the bottom heap on top of the middle, and the middle on top of the top. Give the entire pack a few cuts and exchange packs as you did before. Then each of you look through the other's pack and find the card that you took from your *own*. Lay these cards face down, side by side, then let anyone turn them up at the same time. To the amazement of the onlookers, the two cards match exactly!

Simplicity is the key that makes this trick a real baffler. In shuffling and exchanging packs a few times, you easily note the bottom card of one pack—say, a red-backed pack—before receiving his blue-backed pack. You immediately cut his pack in three heaps by lifting off two thirds and placing it to the right; then lifting off the top third and placing it still farther to the right. Tell him to do the same, so you can each peek at the top card of your middle heap.

In gathering the heaps by dropping the middle on the center and both on top, your partner automatically puts the card you looked at—say, the 5 of spades —on the card he peeked at—say, the jack of diamonds. You only pretend to peek at the card on the middle heap of the pack he gave to you. After you each cut the pack a few times, exchange packs again. All you have to do is look through your pack and find the card you saw on the bottom, namely the 5 of spades, and draw out the card below it, which will be the jack of diamonds, which is the card he peeked at.

While you are placing his card face down on the table, your friend will be looking through your pack for that very same card—the jack of diamonds—so it will automatically match yours when both are turned up together!

ALTERNATE DO AS I DO

To most observers, this looks exactly like the standard Do as I Do with two packs, but from your standpoint, it has two important differences.

First, instead of noting the bottom card of your pack, push the top card an inch or so over the end of the pack and note it by tilting the faces toward you. Square the pack face-down, so that your known card—say, the 5 of spades—is on top of the red-backed pack when the spectator receives it.

Next, in taking the spectator's pack and cutting it in three heaps, you cut it by lifting off two thirds of the pack and placing it well to the right, so you can lift off the top third of the pack and set it in the middle. Since you tell the spectator to do exactly as you do, the 5 of spades will be the top card of the red-backed heap that he looks at—namely, the heap now in the middle. You only pretend to peek at the top card of your blue-backed middle heap.

Actually, you have forced the 5 of spades on the spectator, so if he wants to shuffle the red-backed pack before returning it, you can obligingly shuffle the blue-backed pack and invite him to "do as you do." So when he starts looking for the red-backed 5 of spades, you go after the very same blue-backer and both are turned up together.

THREE-HEAP DO AS I DO

This is an elaboration of the basic Do as I Do. Here three spectators each take a card from a different heap, yet you amazingly match all three after the packs have been exchanged. To do this, you must note and remember the three top cards of your pack, which is really not difficult if you use this as a follow-up to some lesser trick, in which you used a limited number of cards, such as the kings and queens.

Thus in replacing those cards in your pack, you could put the QH, QS, and QC on the top just as they are. Then, giving the spectator your red-backers in exchange for his blues, you start dealing cards in three face-down heaps—left, center, right—telling him to do the same. That puts your key cards on the bottom of each heap, so you can speed things by dealing the cards in clumps from then on.

Have each person look at the top card of a heap and leave it there, while you pretend to do the same. Then gather heaps in any order, giving the pack a few single cuts. Switch packs and have each person look for his card and remove it, while you are finding all three cards, since each will be directly beneath a different key card.

DO AS I DO KNOT

This is a standout among Do as I Do effects, because it causes people to concentrate so intently on what they are doing that they are sure to overlook your added touch—which, of course, is the key to the trick. So it should really read, Do as I Do *Not*.

Hand out a five-foot string or light rope to your audience and show them with your own exactly how to form the rope into a double loop. Then let the loop drop and a knot appears in the center; but when they copy your action, they do not get a knot. Your guests will soon be frustrated because no matter how many times they try, it just won't work.

Basically, this is the same as the Drop-away Knot described on page 26, but in this case you show exactly how the rope is worked into a double loop (Figs. 1, 2, and 3 of Drop-away Knot), making sure that everybody copies you exactly. Now, in bending the hands inward and downward with a forward tilt, you secretly grip the rope with the third and fourth fingers of your right hand just below the loop and release the end of the rope with your thumb and first two fingers (Fig. 4).

The result is automatic. The unseen move causes a knot to form in the center of your rope (Fig. 5), something that no one else will duplicate. If done with ease and complete confidence your guests will never realize you've done something extra.

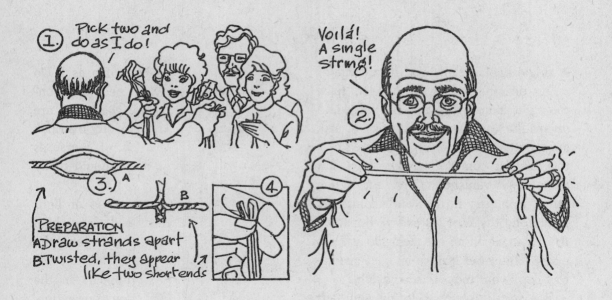

DO AS I DO STRING TRICK

For this baffler, you use a dozen or more pieces of cotton string, each approximately six inches long. Hand these out in pairs to several spectators, keeping a pair for yourself (Fig. 1). Telling other people to "Do as I Do," bundle your two strings into a loose ball and give two of the ends a sudden tug. To everyone's amazement—except yours!—your two short pieces suddenly unite into a single long string (Fig. 2). But when they try to do the same with theirs, they wind up with two "shorties" just as they began.

Use a cheap cotton string for this trick, the type that is formed of long, thin strands, actually consisting of thin strings twisted together. The pairs of six-inchers that you give to your friends are quite ordinary; but your "pair" is actually a twelve-inch length that you have faked to look like two six-inch pieces. To do this, spread the twelve-inch string at the very center, drawing the strands apart to form two small loops (Fig. 3A). Twist these separately to look like two short ends (Fig. 3B) so that when you hold the join between your thumb and forefinger, you apparently have a pair of six-inch strings like everybody else's.

Then proceed to gather up the strings, lightly compressing them together. When you have bundled them sufficiently, take hold of the long ends and give a quick, hard pull. The false short ends will instantly be drawn back to where they belong, giving you a single string that can be examined.

SLIDE-AWAY KNOT

A single knot is tied in a short piece of string or rope, which is dangled from the right hand (Fig. 1). The left hand grasps the knot and draws it downward, apparently tightening it, but instead, as the left fist comes clear, the knot has completely vanished (Fig. 2). When other people try it, they find themselves tightening the knot instead of vanishing it. This makes it an excellent Do as I Do effect. Hand out strings and let spectators copy your moves, to no avail.

The secret is when closing your left fist around the knot, keep the back of the hand toward the spectators and secretly insert the two middle fingers in the loop. Keep spreading the fingers as you draw the loop downward and it will run off the end of the string (Fig. 3). Anyone unfamiliar with this method will snarl the knot instead. Use a smooth string or ribbon or a thin nylon rope and you can repeat the trick time after time, with the same baffling result.

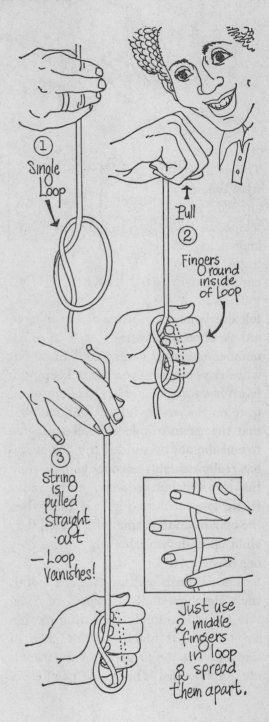

① Single Loop

Pull

② Fingers round inside of Loop

③ String is pulled straight out — Loop Vanishes!

Just use 2 middle fingers in loop & spread them apart.

CALL FOR THE WIZARD

This is a popular form of a "telephone trick" where you invite a friend to name any card in the pack, then talk over the telephone to a mysterious mind reader known as "The Wizard," who concentrates and tells your friend the very card he has in mind.

To add a little showmanship first, tell everyone how marvelous The Wizard is; then say that you will call his number and ask for him, but that you will let your friend do all the talking. Everybody in the room must concentrate on the same thought to make sure that the message is projected, and also to corroborate the fact that The Wizard has really caught the thought—which in this test will be a card named by your friend.

Suppose your friend chooses the 9 of clubs. Dial the number and when someone answers, simply say: "Let me talk to The Wizard." A few moments later, say, "Here he is," and hand the phone to your friend, who asks the name of his card. And The Wizard's reply comes through in mystic tone: "The 9 of clubs!"

Here's how you work it. There is only one person at the other end and he is a confederate who is awaiting your call. When he answers the phone, he starts saying, in a low tone just for you: "Diamonds—hearts—clubs—spades." Since the card is a club, you stop him on that suit by saying, "Let me talk to The Wizard."

In the same low tone, he starts reciting: "Ace—king—queen—jack—10—9—" and you stop him there by saying, "Here's The Wizard" and handing the phone to your friend, who began by naming the 9 of clubs. Of course, The Wizard could continue counting clear down to 2, if necessary; but wherever you stop him he knows that that is the value of the card.

FINGER FIGURES

This starts like a game, but winds up as a mystery. Have two people hold out their right fists, while you turn your back. Each is then to extend some of his fingers, representing a number from 1 to 4, or spread his hand for 5, or even keep his fist closed for 0. Another person, who is acting as referee, calls out the total number of fingers shown and after a few moments of concentration, you name the number of fingers shown by each individual player.

Not only are you right, but you can also repeat the procedure time after time, leaving people more and more bewildered the longer it goes on, even though you may change players on occasion.

You need a partner for this feat, but the system is so neat that you can explain it to a new helper in a few minutes. You tell your partner, Joe, to start by showing three fingers, so if the referee calls "7" as the total, you automatically know that the other player, Andy, is showing 4. On the next turn, Joe is to show the number that Andy has just shown; in this case, 4. That applies to all the numbers that follow, enabling you to keep on and on—and on!—without a miss.

Here is a simple example:

The referee calls: "7." You say: "Joe—3; Andy—4."
The referee calls: "9." You say: "Joe—4; Andy—5."
The referee calls: "6." You say: "Joe—5; Andy—1."
The referee calls: "5." You say: "Joe—1; Andy—4."
The referee calls: "4." You say: "Joe—4; Andy—0."
The referee calls: "2." You say: "Joe—0; Andy—2."
The referee calls: "7." You say: "Joe—2; Andy—5."

Most people look for some signal between you and one of the players, or even the referee, never suspecting that the total itself gives you the cue. When working with a group, other people may be eager to participate, so you can let somebody take Andy's place, but not Joe's, because he is your partner. However:

With a large group, you can always have another partner—perhaps Mary—who can be so eager to get into the game, that you finally let her take Joe's place. Since Mary knows the system, she picks up from where Joe left off and you go right on naming totals. Since this is supposedly a test in ESP, you can always reject a player who does not have the right "vibrations," or you can decide that you have concentrated long enough and call a halt right there.

With a fairly large group, you can introduce a very neat switch. Starting with Joe as a confederate and Andy as a skeptic, you have someone replace Andy and then get Mary—your other confederate—to replace Joe. While the game goes on, Joe has a chance to draw Andy aside and tell him how the trick works. Shortly afterward, Andy becomes anxious to get back in the game, so you let him replace Mary. Thus Andy, the avowed skeptic, a person you never even met before, becomes your secret helper, leaving other skeptics utterly nonplused!

CHAPTER SIX: Mental Magic and Messages

Joseph Dunninger

FOR MANY YEARS, the Eden Musée, on West Twenty-third Street in New York City, was a Mecca of Magic. Its vast array of life-sized waxwork figures included an automatic checker player that would beat you every time you played a game with it. The museum also had a small theater called Egyptian Hall, where such famous magicians as De Kolta, Powell, and Baldwin had appeared for extended engagements. During Christmas week in 1913, I visited the Eden Musée and witnessed a memorable magic show. That may seem like a long while ago, but actually it was only shortly before the museum concluded its thirty-year stay in Manhattan and moved to Coney Island in Brooklyn.

By then, the old-time magicians had come and gone. But the up-and-coming performer who supplanted the old-timers presented such effects as the Chinese Rice Bowls, the Linking Rings, and the Floating Lady, which were becoming well known even then. Among these, he interspersed some specialties of his own, thus rounding out a flawless program. I saw his show again several months later, and he had added other novelties for the benefit of steady customers, which was why he filled a continuous engagement of sixty-five weeks—a record for a magician in New York.

This talented magician's name was Dunninger, and he went on to set far bigger records during the sixty-odd years that I knew him; and during that time, he told me exactly how it all came about for him.

After leaving the Eden Musée, Dunninger began doing private shows along with occasional vaudeville engagements, augmenting his

91

JOSEPH DUNNINGER

skill at sleight-of-hand with some large tricks and illusions requiring three or four assistants. All the while, he was buying up larger and heavier equipment, moving toward a full-scale magic show that would rival the biggest in the business, until one eventful evening changed his plans entirely.

Dunninger had finished a stage show at a private club and his assistants were packing up when the chairman of the club's entertainment committee stopped by and asked him to do more of his skillful work for the benefit of some special guests. Dunninger agreed, but rather than repeat his expert manipulations with coins and cards, he had members of the audience write names and numbers on slips of paper; then called them off, to everyone's amazement. Instead of having them take cards from a pack, he had them simply think of cards, yet he proceeded to find them and produce them from unexpected places, leaving them utterly dumfounded.

"I was doing magic," Dunninger told me, "but they didn't know it. If I changed a silver half dollar into a twenty-dollar gold piece and back again, they were sure it had to be a trick, no matter how completely I fooled them. But if I switched a folded paper for a duplicate, then opened the original and read it before switching it back, they thought I was reading their minds."

Apparently, Dunninger himself didn't immediately realize the effect he was having. A few weeks later, his agent received a call from the club where he had appeared, saying they wanted him there again.

When the agent reminded them that they had seen Dunninger only a few weeks before, the committee man said, "We don't mean his regular stage show, we mean his new show. Everybody who has heard about it wants to see it." The agent promptly phoned Dunninger demanding to know why he was booking a new act on his own; and in reply, Dunninger could only ask, with real surprise, "What act?"

When the agent named the client, Dunninger was able to explain that he had simply put on a brief act as a courtesy to the chairman, but since they liked it so well, he would be willing to expand it. So the agent called the club and booked Dunninger for a date at his full fee. During the interim, he developed further effects in mental magic, and on the appointed night, instead of bringing a truckload of illusions and a crew of assistants, Dunninger arrived with a suitcase containing pads, pencils, envelopes, chalk, slates, playing cards, and other commonplace items, which he used to demonstrate what he termed "Miracles of the Mind."

From then on, the new act steadily replaced the old, with constantly increasing bookings at fees that grew with the demand. Such success simply furthered Dunninger's urge to go on tour with a full-evening magic show, and ten years after he had left the Eden Musée, he achieved that ambition. He appeared from coast to coast, carrying a company that approached the size of Thurston's. Along with magic and illusions, he presented his one-man mental act on an elaborate scale, distributing pads, pencils, and envelopes throughout the audience; then answering questions from the stage without having assistants gather them.

I saw Dunninger's big show in the Philadelphia Metropolitan Opera House, the largest theater in the city (a vast contrast to the compact Egyptian Hall of New York's Eden Musée, which is a good example of what had been going on throughout the country). We all expected him to go out the next season with a still bigger show, but his fame as a mentalist had reached New York ahead of him and he was booked for private engagements at such fabulous fees that he put his big show in storage, even selling some of his best equipment to Houdini, who was going out with a road show of his own.

For nearly twenty years, Dunninger continued his phenomenal career, performing at exclusive clubs and elite social events, which included several appearances at the White House. I saw him frequently during those years and worked with him on articles, books, and radio scripts. With theater business falling off, Dunninger regarded his big show as a relic of the past, and his new ambition was to go on the air with his one-man act. I handled the final arrangements for his initial broadcast from Station KYW in Philadelphia, and its success led to his regular program from WJZ in New York, over a national network.

The result was so sensational that from then on Dunninger starred in radio, usually "warming up" with a "live" audience before going on. This created a demand for public appearances, which he filled between his broadcasting commitments. When television overtook radio, Dunninger's popularity increased, since his act had become visual, and the reactions of the baffled spectators whose minds he apparently read added to the excitement. In all, Dunninger covered a twenty-five-year period on radio and TV before he finally retired. By then, he had set the pace for a whole new trend in mental magic, so that today there are literally hundreds of self-styled "mentalists" in the field.

Analyzing this, we find that many feats of mentalism are mere magical effects that appear to be a "thought coincidence" rather than the result of skill or trickery. Here is an example that Dunninger frequently demonstrated to prove that very point, one that you can try for yourself:

Give a pack of cards to a spectator, tell him to shuffle it and meanwhile think of a number, anywhere from 1 up to 15, without naming it. That done, have him turn his back and count off that many cards from the top of the pack, putting them in his pocket. Then tell him to count off the same number again; but this time, he is to turn the group to himself and note the bottom card, the one facing his way. Add that he is to remember that card and replace the group squarely on the pack, then give you the pack, face down.

Holding the pack in your left hand, ask three other persons each to give you a man's first name, specifying that it must be an actual name, not just a nickname. Assuming that the names are Richard, George, and Arthur, you proceed to spell those names by dealing cards, one for each letter, so that they form a pile on the table, each card going on the one before. Call the letters as you spell them, so there can be no mistake; then gather up the entire heap and replace it on the pack.

Now tell those three helpers: "I want each of you to spell the name you chose, exactly as I showed you, but now we will use the full pack." With that you give the pack to the man who had it originally and tell him to bring out the cards from his pocket and replace them on the pack. Up to that point, nothing could be more fair and above board; if any trickery is due, it will have to come after you take the pack again. But you don't even touch the pack from then on.

Instead, you have the holder give it to the helper who named "Richard" so he can spell R-I-C-H-A-R-D, dealing a card for each letter. It then goes to the second helper, who spells out "G-E-O-R-G-E," and finally the third helper, who completes the spelling with "A-R-T-H-U-R." He then lays the pack in the center of the table, while you turn to the man who held the pack originally and sum the situation with this statement:

"I have no idea what number you chose originally. Nor is it possible for me to know what card you looked at. These other three people had free choice of the names they gave me and they spelled them out themselves, so whatever happens now will be a meeting of the minds —your minds, not mine." Pointing to the pack, you add: "I want you to take the top card from the pack and hold it face down." As he does, you say, "Now name the card you looked at."

He names it; for example: "The jack of spades."

You tell him: "Turn the card face up."

He turns it up. It *is* the jack of spades!

Follow the procedure exactly as given and you will find that this amazing effect works itself automatically. You can practice it with imaginary people: One handling the pack to start, the others spelling chosen names. But don't omit that part where you deal the cards yourself, showing them how the names are to be spelled. That reverses the order of the cards then on top of the pack and that does the trick!

Just one more point: The names that are chosen must total more than fifteen letters in order to be safe. So if you are given three short names, like Roy, Ira, and Wayne, simply turn to a fourth person and ask him to give you another name, thus raising the total. It doesn't make a bit of difference what number the original person decides to use, provided it isn't more than the specified fifteen!

THE COUNTING RACE

This is a fast-moving game that has a trick to it, so that you can always win. Tell a person to pick any number from 1 to 10, naming it aloud; let's say, 8. To that, you add a number from 1 to 10 inclusive—say, 6—naming 14 as your total. Continue in that fashion, with 10 as your limit, and whoever hits 100 is winner of the race.

The trick is this: By hitting 89, you can always win, as your opponent must name at least 1, but no more than 10. So 89 becomes a vital "key number," which in turn is controlled by lesser "keys" running 1, 12, 23, 34, 45, 56, 67, and 78, which are easily remembered because each is just 11 more than the one before. Aim for one of those "keys"—say, 56—and you have 100 in the bag. Take this example, in which the totals in italics are your calls: 3, *10*, 16, *20*, 30, *36*, 37, *38*, 47, *56*, 60, *67*, 77, *78*, 85, *89*, 90, *100*.

Of course, the sooner you hit a key number, the earlier you clinch the game. This means that any time you have the "first call" you can win the game at the very start by naming 3 and following with every key number from then on to 100.

NAMING NUMBERS

For a "two person" effect, this can prove highly baffling, yet it is very easily learned and therefore specially suited to younger performers. One person, who is to play the part of a "mind reader," leaves the room, while the other, who acts as the "subject," is given a number —say, from 1 to 15—by the members of the audience.

The subject stands facing the spectators while the mind reader is called into the room. Without a word passing between them, the mind reader steps in back of the subject and extends his hands, placing his fingertips on the subject's temples. Slowly, the mind reader counts aloud: "1—2—3—" and so on, until he comes to the chosen number, when he stops and says, "That's it!" This may be repeated time and again, yet always, the mind reader will hit the number correctly.

Actually, the subject signals the number to the mind reader, but the method is so neatly hidden that no one can observe it. When the mind reader has counted to the chosen number—say, 9—the subject simply presses his teeth tightly together. This action, slight though it is, produces an outward pressure at the subject's temples, which is easily noted by the mind reader. He claims that he is "sensing the subject's pulsation" in order to "obtain a mental impression," and many people really think he does, which makes the trick all the better.

NAMING THE OBJECT

Here is a feat of pretended "thought projection" with a reverse twist that makes it utterly baffling to the average onlooker. As in other tricks of this type, two people are involved: One who projects the thought, the "sender," and another who acts as "receiver" and picks up the impression correctly.

The receiver stands with his back to the audience, pressing his arm across his eyes and resting it against the wall, so that he cannot possibly see what is going on. The sender asks the spectators to point to any object in the room, such as a coffee table, so he can project the thought to the receiver. He then points to various objects in slow progression, asking, "Is it the sofa?" "Is it the radio?" "Is it the wastebasket?" always getting "No" for an answer until he asks, "Is it the coffee table?" and then he gets a prompt "Yes" from the receiver.

This can be repeated, with the spectators choosing a different object; and again, with smaller items, such as a cigarette, a coin, a pencil—always with the same success. If the spectators suspect that the sender is changing his tone, he can simply point to each item, letting anyone ask, "Is this it?" without even naming the object. Yet the receiver will name the chosen object every time, and the closer the spectators watch the sender, the less chance they have of guessing the secret.

That is because they will be looking for some sort of signal on the sender's part, although there is actually none at all!

That is where the reverse twist comes in. The receiver is the one who gives the signal. The sender starts by pointing to any object except the chosen one, and when asked if it is the object, the receiver simply says "No." The sender picks another wrong object and the receiver supplies another "No." Finally, just after again saying "No," the receiver raises his arm very slightly against the wall, and the sender, spotting that action, names the chosen object or points to it on his next turn.

Nobody suspects a signal from the receiver, who is supposedly playing a strictly passive part. It is natural for the sender to glance toward the receiver after naming an object, or pointing to one, so the fact that he is picking up a cue for the next object is almost certain to be overlooked. Getting someone to work as the receiver is easy, as you can explain the system very quickly. Then, posing as the sender, you can baffle your audience with a helper whom you apparently picked at random.

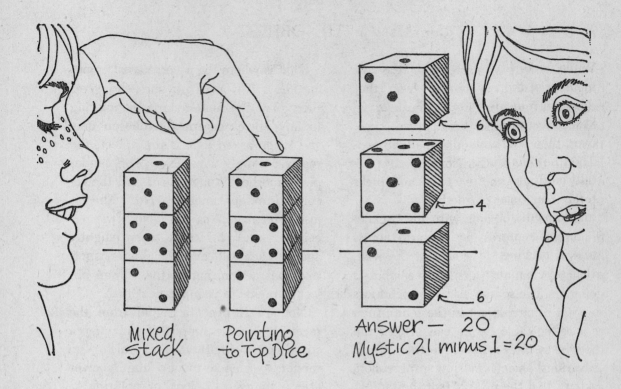

Mixed Stack

Pointing to Top Dice

Answer — 20
Mystic 21 minus 1 = 20

MYSTIC TOTALS

While your back is turned have someone put three dice in a stack. Facing the spectators, call attention to the fact that five sides of the dice are completely hidden—that is, the bottom of the uppermost die and the tops and bottoms of the two dice below. By simply touching the visible side of the top die you can name the total of the five hidden sides.

The secret to this trick is simple.

Since the opposite sides of a pair of dice always total seven, the opposite sides of three dice will always add up to twenty-one. By subtracting the number on the uppermost die of the stack from twenty-one you get the total of the five hidden sides. Example: If a 1 shows on top, the total is 20, as in the illustration. If a 5 shows on top, the total of the hidden sides is 16. Simple mental arithmetic.

ROLL THE DICE

While your back is turned tell a member of the audience to roll a pair of dice and remember the total; then have him pick up one of the dice and turn it over, then add the number on that side. Then he rolls that same cube and mentally adds its number to obtain a final total. You turn and face the spectator and immediately name the grand total.

As an example, the spectator rolls 3 and 2, totaling 5. He picks up the die that says 2 and turns it over, adding 5,

which is the number on the other side. Now he has 10.

He rolls the cube again: It registers 1, which when added makes 11. You, looking at the dice, see the original 3 and the 1, which add up to 4. All you have to do is add 7 and announce the grand total, which is 11. This never fails if instructions are followed. Remember to always add 7 to the amount shown on the two dice when you turn around.

START

① ← 3+2=5 → ②

But only 🎲 and 🎲 are visible

Turn Over

#2

5 = 10 + 1 = 11

Roll the 🎲 again

99

CIRCLES AND SQUARES

This mental mystery involves a few special items that can be easily prepared. First you'll need five circles measuring about three inches in diameter, cut from thin cardboard. On each of these, inscribe a number of four figures around the rim of the circle, leaving space enough to show where the number begins and ends. The numbers are: 3 8 5 2, 4 3 8 5, 2 4 3 8, 5 2 4 3, 8 5 2 4.

On five cardboard squares, measuring two inches each way, inscribe the same numbers, one to each card (Fig. 1).

Begin the trick by checking the circles against the square, pointing out that their numbers correspond. Mixing the circles, put them in your pocket or beneath a handkerchief; then draw out one at random and hold it with the numbered side downward. Then have someone else take the squares, draw one, and lay it on the table with its number up. Assuming his square to be 4 3 8 5, you turn up your circle, point to its figures, and show that it, too, is 4 3 8 5, the very same number! (Fig. 2).

This can be repeated, always with the same success, due to a special device that no one suspects. That device is an *extra circle*, bearing *five* figures instead of only *four*; namely, 3 8 5 2 4, completing the circle (Fig. 3). This cir-

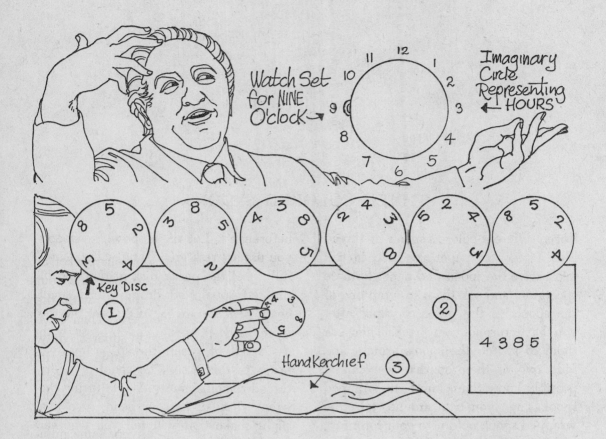

cle is already in your pocket or under the handkerchief before you conceal the five ordinary circles. The one you bring out is the *extra*, and when the spectator turns up a square card, you note its number—as, 4 3 8 5—and put your thumb over the unneeded figure on your circular card, in this case 2, so that your number 4 3 8 5 will be the same as his.

Following that, you simply slide the special disk in with the others and you can either repeat the trick or conclude it by putting all the disks away.

THREE COLORED SPOOLS

Three different-colored spools of thread plus a piece of paper are used in this trick. Give the spools and paper to three spectators and ask them to wrap one of the spools in the piece of paper after you have turned your back. Then ask them to switch the spools around and hide two of them so that you cannot possibly know the color of the wrapped spool. Then you turn around, take the wrapped spool, hold it to your forehead, and immediately name the color of the thread.

You must prepare two of the spools beforehand. Let us suppose the spools you use are red, green, and white. Carefully peel the paper disk at one end of the red spool and drop in one small bead. Seal the paper disk back in the same place. Repeat this process with the spool of green thread, using two beads in this case. The spool of white thread remains empty. While lifting the wrapped spool to your head, give it a slight shake that will tell you whether you have the empty white spool, or the red spool with one bead, or the green spool with two beads.

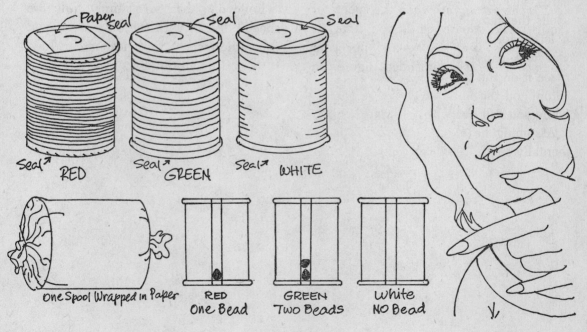

One Spool Wrapped in Paper   RED One Bead   GREEN Two Beads   White NO Bead

CHOOSE A PLANET

Take five blank cards and on each draw a picture of a planet, according to astrology, adding the names that identify them: Moon, Venus, Saturn, and Jupiter. You can also include the Sun (Fig. 1). Spread these on a table and let a person choose a planet without telling you which one he takes. Promptly gather the cards, keeping the faces toward you, and form a little packet, which you turn face down.

Then state that you will draw off cards one by one while the chooser spells the name of his planet, mentally, a letter for each card. You state that you will pause with each card, then place it on the bottom, but he is to say, "Stop!" on the final letter of his planet, while you still have that card in hand.

Assuming he chooses Venus, he will mentally spell "V-e-n-u-s" and then add

"Stop!" while you are holding the fifth card. Turning that card face up, you show it to be the planet Venus!

This trick works automatically, because each planet has just one more letter than the card ahead of it. Gather the cards in the order Saturn, Jupiter, Sun, Moon, Venus, running from the top of the face-down packet downward, and the chooser is sure to hit on whatever name he spells.

A good suggestion is to make up other cards as substitutes for those already listed: Mars for Moon, Pluto for Venus, Uranus for Saturn, Mercury or Neptune for Jupiter. That helps if you repeat the trick, as the substitution of new names seems to widen the choice, although it actually works out just the same.

THREE CLOCK TRICKS

Here are three tricks that can be worked individually, alternately, or in combination, using a simple drawing of a clock dial numbered from 1 to 12, and a pencil. Make the diameter of the dial just about the length of the pencil and put a large dot in the center. You are now ready to proceed.

CROSSWISE SUBTRACTION While your back is turned have someone lay the pencil across the clock dial so that it covers the center dot and crosses two numbers on the dial, one large and the other small. Tell the person to subtract the small number from the large and take away the pencil. Looking at the dial, you give the result of his subtraction.

This works automatically. Opposite numbers on a clock dial always reduce to 6 when the lesser is subtracted from the greater. Thus 12—6=6; 11—5=6; 10—4=6; and so on. You just can't miss, which makes it a good trick.

AROUND THE DIAL In this test, the pencil is simply used to count around the dial, beginning at No. 1 and counting to the right, to any number that the person wants—say, 10—without telling you. Then, starting with No. 12, he is to count around the same number to the left, which means that in this case, he would stop on 3. He adds those totals: 10+3=13, and keeps it in mind while you study the dial and come up with the result: 13. Try it and you will find that it always works.

CROSS OUT SIX In this variation of Around the Dial you tell someone to cross out No. 6 entirely; then count around to the left and stop at a number—say, 2—and remember it. His count, in this case, would run: 7, 8, 9, 10, 11, 12, 1, 2—making eight counts in all.

Again, starting from the crossed-out 6, he is to make the same number of counts, this time to the *right*, and note the number on which he stops. Thus his count would run 5, 4, 3, 2, 1, 12, 11, 10, eight counts in all, stopping at No. 10, which he also notes. Then have him add those numbers mentally and keep the total in mind, unless it happens to be the same, in which case he is to concentrate on the number itself. He does this; and you come up with the answer: 12!

Like the other clock tricks this one works itself, as the only possible combinations are $7+5=12$; $8+4=12$; $9+3=12$; $10+2=12$; $11+1=12$; and 12 itself. You can tell a person to count as high as he wants—to 20, 30, or even more in each direction, simply skipping the crossed-out 6 if he goes that far.

By switching from one of these devices to another, you can apparently repeat the clock test for the same group, but always with a different result, making it all the more effective.

Example "A"

SUN	MON	TUE	WED	THUR	FRI	SAT
1	2	3	4	~~5~~	6	7
8	9	10	11	12	13	~~14~~
15	16	17	18	~~19~~	20	21
22	23	24	~~25~~	26	27	28
29	~~30~~	31				

Example "A"
30 + 25 + 5 + 19 + 14 = 93

Example "B"

SUN	MON	TUES	WED	THUR	FRI	SAT
			~~1~~	2	3	4
5	6	7	8	9	~~10~~	11
~~12~~	13	14	15	16	17	18
19	20	21	~~22~~	23	24	25
26	27	28	29	~~30~~	31	

Example "B"
12 + 1 + 22 + 30 + 10 = 75

CALENDAR CALCULATION

This highly impressive effect requires some careful calculation, but after you have tried it several times, it will come naturally and easily, much to the mystification of your audience. Use a monthly calendar that has either thirty or thirty-one days (which eliminates February), but make sure that the first day of the month is a Sunday, Monday, Tuesday, Wednesday, or Thursday; not a Friday or Saturday. This means that the dates will carry into a fifth week, but not into a sixth.

While your back is turned, tell someone to cross out one date in each week, making five crossed-off dates in all. That done, ask him how many Sundays he has crossed out; then how many Mondays; how many Tuesdays; and so on. Since you don't ask in which week these days appear, it is obvious that you have no way of knowing or even guessing the exact dates. But at the finish, you tell the person to add the five dates and write the total on a piece of paper, whereupon you name the total —say, 93!—and your total proves to be correct!

Two factors are responsible for this surprising result. Any month that you use has a "basic total" dependent on the day of the week on which the month begins. If the first is a Sunday, your basic total will be 75; for a Monday, 70; for a Tuesday, 65; for a Wednesday, 60; for a Thursday, 55. To that total, you add 0 for each Sunday that the person crosses off; 1 for each Monday; 2 for each Tuesday; 3 for each Wednesday; 4 for each Thursday; 5 for each Friday; and 6 for each Saturday.

In Example A, where the first is a Sunday, your basic total is 75. Keeping that in mind, you add the values of the days of the week as the person calls them off: 1 for a Monday; 3 for a Wednesday; 8 for two Thursdays; and 6 for a Saturday. This makes a total of $75+1+3+8+6=93$.

In Example B, the first is a Wednesday, giving you 60 for a basic total. Adding the crossed-off days, you have 0 for a Sunday; 6 for two Wednesdays; 4 for a Thursday; and 5 for a Friday. This gives you $60+0+6+4+5=75$.

This is an excellent repeat trick, because you can use a variety of monthly sheets, making it hard for people to figure out the system. Since different people will cross off different days, the totals also vary in each case.

THE THREE NUMBERS

Ask a spectator to write down three one-digit numbers. Any number from 0 to 9 will do and can be used more than once if desired. You do not see the numbers. Next ask him to double the first number, add three, then multiply by five. To this he adds the second number and multiplies the total by 10. To that total he adds the third number, then adds fifteen. Have the spectator name the final total. After you have heard the sum, you tell him the very three numbers that he originally wrote, each in its proper order.

Always be sure to give the proper instructions. When you learn the sum total, deduct 165. You will then have a number of three figures, from left to right; those figures will be the ones that the person selected at the start.

EXAMPLE: NUMBERS 8–1–3
8 doubled=16.   Add 3=19.
Multiply by 5 which makes   95
Add 2nd number (1) making   96
Multiply by 10 making   960
Add 3rd number (3) making   963
Add 15 forming total of   978
Secretly subtract   165
Three original numbers   813

MAGIC MATH

This rates high among prediction tricks, if carefully followed. Have someone write a number of three *different* figures; for example, 387. He is then to *reverse* that number, which would be 783; then write it down so that he can subtract the smaller number from the larger. For example:

$$
\begin{array}{r}
783 \\
-387 \\
\hline
396
\end{array}
$$

Now he is to reverse that result, write it underneath, and add the two together:

$$
\begin{array}{r}
396 \\
+693 \\
\hline
1089
\end{array}
$$

Without a glance at the paper, or even a blink of an eye, you state the total: 1089. Amazingly, you are right! Follow the procedure given and the result will always be 1089—that is, if you avoid one pitfall. When the person is doing his subtraction, tell him:

"If the result in under 100—say, a number like 28 or 43—put a 0 in front of it, making it 028 or 043, so you will still have a number of three figures."

That takes care of an occasional calculation that would otherwise go wrong. For example:

$$
\begin{array}{r}
615 \\
-516 \text{ (reversed)} \\
\hline
099
\end{array}
\qquad
\begin{array}{r}
099 \\
+990 \text{ (reversed)} \\
\hline
1089
\end{array}
$$

SUPER MATH

As a follow-up or alternate for Magic Math, this effect is ideal, because it always has a different result, and almost no one acquainted with the original trick will recognize it in this more elaborate form. It also requires more careful calculation, so make sure to pick a person who is fond of addition and subtraction.

Have someone write down a number of five *different* figures; reverse the number, and subtract the smaller from the larger.

You then say: "If the result has only *four* figures, put a zero in front of it. If it has *five* figures, let it stand as it is." Pause briefly and continue: "Now write the result in reverse and add them both together."

With a *four*-figure result, here is a sample of the final total:

$$
\begin{array}{r} 34862 \\ -26843 \\ \hline 8019 \end{array}
\qquad
\begin{array}{r} 08019 \\ +91080 \\ \hline 99099 \end{array}
$$

With a *five*-figure result, the reversal may lead to this addition:

$$
\begin{array}{r} 64583 \\ -38546 \\ \hline 26037 \end{array}
\qquad
\begin{array}{r} 26037 \\ +73062 \\ \hline 99099 \end{array}
$$

However, the final total is not yet certain, so to clinch it, you then ask:

"Don't tell me your number; just tell me how many figures it has—five or six—so I can concentrate and call them off mentally." If the person says that the number has five figures, you announce the total slowly, figure by figure: "9—9—0—9—9!" You will be right. It's always 99099.

However, there is a type that works differently:

$$
\begin{array}{r} 98431 \\ -13489 \\ \hline 84942 \end{array}
\qquad
\begin{array}{r} 84942 \\ +24948 \\ \hline 109890 \end{array}
$$

So if the person who did the adding says that there are six figures in the total, you simply call them off accordingly—1—0—9—8—9—0—and you are right.

SQUARE OF NINE

Using any monthly calendar, while your back is turned have someone mark a square consisting of nine dates. That done, the person should call out the number of the lowest date in the square —say, 5. Going into a "mood of calculation," you come up with a formidable total, such as 117. When your friend carefully adds all the numbers in the square of nine, it turns out that your total was right. This can be repeated, using dates from any month a person chooses, yet always your answer will be correct.

It all depends on a fairly simple calculation. Add 8 to the date named; multiply that number by 10, simply by putting on a 0; and subtract the number itself. That will give you the total of the square. In the example given, this would run:

$$5+8=13\times10=130-13=117$$

Repeating the trick with a different month adds to the effect, because the blocks of nine are apt to vary according to the day of the week on which the month starts. This makes the trick appear more difficult, but actually the formula is the same, as shown in the second example:

$$10+8=18\times10=180-18=162$$

CHAPTER SEVEN: Money Magic

Horace Goldin

GOLDIN'S DOLLAR-BILL TRICK

ON THE NIGHT OF January 29, 1920, I went to the Cross Keys Theater in West Philadelphia to watch the performance of a famous illusionist, Horace Goldin. I had never seen him perform before, but I had heard much about him. Twenty years before, Goldin had created a sensation in the field of magic and in theatrical circles as well by developing a "silent act" in which he presented tricks and illusions in rapid-fire style. He had taken his act to England, where it had gained top billing in London's best vaudeville theaters.

The novelty of viewing a dozen spectacular mysteries in as many minutes left British audiences so bewildered that they had to go to see Goldin's act again and again, just to catch up with it. So Goldin had stayed in England almost continually for a dozen years, changing and expanding his repertoire to keep it fresh and new. Toward the end of 1913 he returned to the United States with his large company and headlined some of the bigger vaudeville circuits. Those of us who failed to see him at that time kept looking forward to his next American tour.

But when Goldin went back to England to fulfill engagements in the summer of 1914, the war in Europe suddenly broke out and he was forced to change his plans entirely. He arranged engagements in India and Australia as "futures," and during the next year, he and his company headed for South Africa en route to the Orient. This developed into what was practically a four-year world tour that brought him back into the United States after the war had ended.

By then, much of Goldin's equipment had been lost or damaged, but he had enough available to put together an act that was suited to the lesser vaudeville circuits, which were doing an expanding business in the wake of World War I. Portions of his act still showed Goldin's famous rapid fire, such as his production of flags of the Allied nations, springing out of nowhere in increasing size and number until they filled the entire stage, culminating in two huge American flags, each complete with a staff.

Goldin deliberately slackened pace when he presented two illusions: One was Walking Through Glass, in which a girl stood on an isolated platform behind a solid sheet of plate glass. A threefold screen was placed at her sides, in back, and another was set up in front of the glass. When the screens were removed, the girl was seen in front of the glass, yet at every moment of the penetration, the glass itself had been visible above, below, and beside the screens.

The other illusion was Goldin's own version of the famous Indian Rope Trick, where he had a boy climb a magically suspended rope to a height of several feet. Then Goldin ascended a tall flight of movable steps and covered the boy with a cloth. As soon as Goldin came down, the steps were wheeled off so that he could reach up and whip away the cloth in the very center of the stage, with no trace of the boy remaining.

Horace Goldin was stocky and rotund in build, not the type that you would normally picture as a magician. But when he "filled in" with fast-moving silent routines, people sat amazed. Whenever Goldin talked, he had a natural wit that brought laughs from the audience. In all, he had a great act, well worth waiting those years to see. Goldin was a man you knew you ought to meet; and I made a point of stopping backstage to see him after a show one night.

The group I was with included James Wobensmith, a patent attorney so deeply versed in magic that some years later he was elected national president of the Society of American Magicians; and also Alvin Plough, a Philadelphia newspaperman who eventually became editor of the *Linking Ring*, the official organ of the International Brotherhood of Magicians. Another of our party, Samuel Paul, was building his own magic show and had brought along his son Leonard, whom we had nicknamed "The Young Herrmann," to see the Great Goldin. Our enthusiasm roused Goldin to such a pitch that he forgot that he had worked three shows that day and accepted Paul's invitation to come over to his house, which was nearby. We were still talking and doing magic, and the get-together didn't break up until nearly four in the morning. That marked the first of many more such meetings while Goldin was appearing at other vaudeville houses in the Philadelphia area.

I would stop backstage to see the Great Goldin at such theaters as the Globe, the Nixon, the Colonial, or the Keystone. What intrigued me about his show was his obvious enjoyment of even the smallest tricks. Often, when we would go out for a cup of coffee, he would take out a dollar bill to pay the check and suddenly tear it in half; then bring his hands together and draw out the bill, fully restored, under the eyes of the astonished cashier!

A year or more later, I saw Goldin frequently in New York, where he was building a new show; and on one occasion, he gave me the details of his "Dollar-bill Tear," which goes as follows:

Spread a dollar bill between your hands, the tips of your fingers at the front corners; the tips of your thumbs in back (Fig. 1). Now bring the left hand to the center of the bill, bending the second finger inward so that it comes in back of the bill (Fig. 2).

Now move the right hand in to meet the left, keeping the right fingers in front, so that they cover the left forefinger (Fig. 3). At that moment, the left forefinger doubles inward, bringing the right half of the bill behind the left fingers. This is shown from your "inside" view (Fig. 4). From the front, however, it appears that the fingers of the right hand have gripped their half of the dollar bill.

The right hand delivers a sharp downward stroke, making a tearing sound as though ripping off its half of the bill (Fig. 5). Actually, it would have done just that if the bill had not been flipped inward by the left forefinger a moment before.

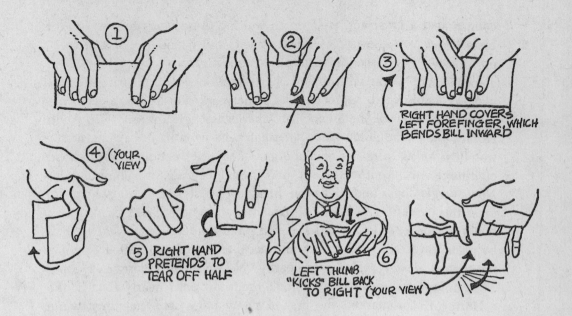

The action is so realistic that when you swing your right hand off to the right, many observers will swear that they saw its share of the bill go with it. To carry that impression still further, slide your left thumb in between the folds of the bill, so when the right hand circles back to meet the left, your left thumb "kicks" the right half of the bill over to the right (Fig. 6).

By spreading the right fingers as their half of the bill arrives behind them, you add to the impression that it was there all the time. And when the hands are drawn apart, spreading the bill between them, it looks exactly as if you were fitting the two halves of a torn bill together.

That was Goldin's short version. He had another that was longer, but had to be performed just as briskly. It goes like this: After "tearing" the bill, the left hand boldly shows its "half," tilting it to an upright position. The empty right hand comes over as though it still held its half, and holds the bill until the left fingers can grip it as before. By simply repeating the former move, you tear the bill into imaginary quarters.

The left hand then extends its "quarter" horizontally, exactly as it did with the original bill (as shown in Fig. 1), and the right hand approaches as before, as if to tear it in eighths. The left forefinger again supplies the necessary "flip" and the hands are separated and brought together, so that then, majestically, you can unfold the entire bill and show it completely restored!

I say "majestically" because that was the way Goldin performed it—like everything else he did. In England, Goldin had fulfilled so many command performances with his big show that he had advertised himself as the "Royal Illusionist," so he felt he had every right to tear an American dollar into halves, quarters, and even eighths—the equivalent of an English sixpence. In England, he had always started with a one-pound note and cut it down proportionately.

Getting back to the trick itself, I suggested a small addition that Horace personally approved as we discussed it over the coffee cups. It was this: Why not fold another dollar bill into halves, quarters, and eighths? Have that already concealed in the bend of the right fingers. Now work the "tear" exactly as Horace did it, but toward the finish press the two bills together so that they could be twisted apart when down to one-eighth size, showing "half" in each hand. You follow that by pretending to squeeze them together, with the right thumb drawing the extra bill back into the finger bend, so it will be hidden there. Then unfold the original bill and show it to be intact.

Hiding the extra bill is quite easy under cover of the outspread original; and both bills can then be pocketed together. This applies even when working with a borrowed bill, as you can pocket it first, then remember that it isn't yours, so you bring it out and return it to its owner, leaving the extra bill in your pocket.

Once, while doing the trick with two crisp ten-dollar bills fresh from the bank, I accidentally tore the original in half at the start. Rather than give up, I showed the halves separately, put one on the other, and went on with the pretended tearing process, folding the torn bill as described, and adding the extra at the finish. I then unfolded the extra instead of the original, which I retained in the finger bend. I handed the unfolded duplicate to a spectator and everybody was so eager to examine it that I had no trouble pocketing the torn bill unnoticed.

As for Goldin, he continued to mingle small tricks with big illusions, claiming that each type gave him ideas for the other. That certainly applied in the case of tearing a bill in half and restoring it. A few years later, he came up with the most sensational illusion of all time, sawing a Woman in Half, which has become a classic, synonymous with magic. Whenever I watched him present it, my thoughts went back to the bill trick.

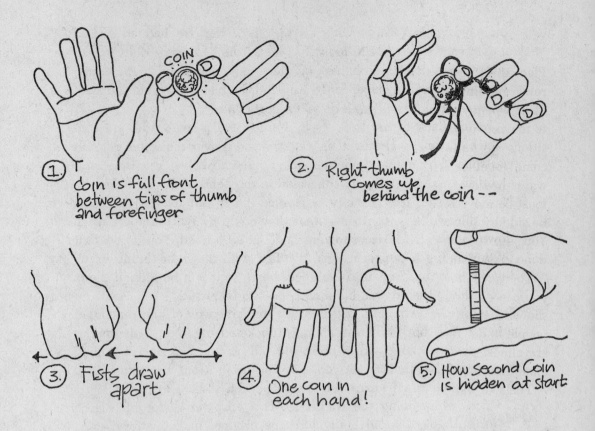

1. Coin is full front between tips of thumb and forefinger

2. Right thumb comes up behind the coin --

3. Fists draw apart

4. One coin in each hand!

5. How second coin is hidden at start

DOUBLE YOUR MONEY

Show a large coin, held between the tips of your left thumb and fingers, which point forward so that everyone can see that the hand is otherwise empty. Your right hand is held open to show that it is also completely empty.

The right hand approaches the left and thrusts its thumb up in back of the coin, so its fingers can close downward over the coin. The left hand closes at the same time and the fists are drawn well apart. You then ask, "Which hand has the coin?" and whichever they say, the answer is "wrong," because you open the *other* hand and show the coin there.

Then, for a real surprise, you open the chosen hand and show another coin there!

The secret is very clever. Set the second coin behind the first so that it points straight backward between the left thumb and second finger, which hide it from the sides while the original coin conceals it from the front (Fig. 5). After showing both hands, which are apparently empty except for the one coin, bring them together and take away the original coin in the right hand while the left retains the duplicate.

116

SIX CENTS AT A TIME

Place three pennies and two nickels in a row, running penny, nickel, penny, nickel, penny. Now challenge someone to move two coins at a time to new positions so that the nickels and pennies come together in separate groups. Always, however, a nickel and a penny must be moved together, and they must be side by side at the start of the move. You also specify that the trick must be done in four such moves.

To prove how easy this should be, you can go through the moves yourself, showing exactly what you expect other people to do. But when they try it, they are almost sure to miss out somewhere along the line, even after you repeat it!

The four moves are as follows:

1. Move the nickel and penny at the right end of the line clear to the left, allowing space for the next two coins.

2. Move the nickel and penny now at the right end of the line to the extreme left.

3. Only one nickel now has a penny just to its left. Move those two coins together to fill the space that you left at the right.

4. Move the nickel and penny from the right of the line to fill the space at the left.

Practice these moves by placing your first two fingers on two adjacent coins, and you can slide each pair smoothly and rapidly, making the moves very difficult to follow. You can also vary the trick by switching to three nickels and two pennies. It will still be "six cents" on each move, but it will confuse onlookers still more.

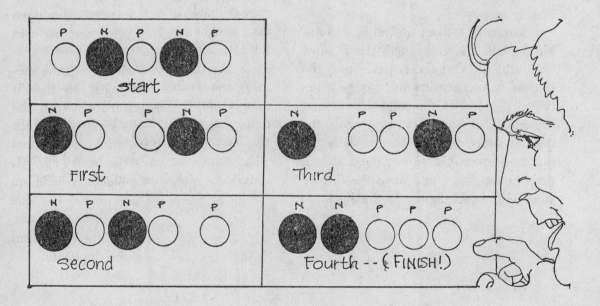

117

① Show DIME

Close matchbox

② Dime is now a QUARTER!

PREPARATION

FALSE BOTTOM   QUARTER   DIME

False bottom drops down covering dime & revealing quarter.

DIME TO QUARTER

Holding a box of safety matches wide open, dump the matches from the drawer; then drop a dime into the drawer and push it shut. With a magic word, you again push the drawer open and the dime has changed into a quarter, which is dropped on the table so the box and drawer can be shown completely empty.

A box with a deep drawer is preferable for this trick, although the shallow type will do. Cut the bottom from the drawer of another box and wedge it between the end of the solid drawer and the cover of the matchbox, with the quarter squeezed in between. Show the box well opened, spill out the matches, drop in the dime, and press the drawer shut with your thumb at the back, so

the false bottom will drop into the drawer, supplanting the dime with the quarter.

Open the box, show the quarter, and remove the drawer entirely, pressing the false bottom with your thumb as you turn over the drawer and let the quarter fall on the table. Push the drawer back into the cover and drop the matchbox in your pocket. Make sure the false bottom is just loose enough to drop into the drawer, but not too loose to be noticeable when you show the drawer empty. Calling attention to the empty cover will distract attention from the "empty" drawer.

A penny can be used instead of the dime, or a nickel instead of a quarter.

QUICK COIN VANISH

Show a dime, place it on the center of a half dollar, and set another half dollar on top, so the dime is sandwiched between the two larger coins, which you hold horizontally between the tips of your right thumb and forefinger (Fig. 1). Extending your left hand palm upward, release the lower half dollar, and when it lands in the left hand, people are surprised to see that the dime is gone. That draws suspicion to the upper half dollar, but you drop it along with the lower half dollar, and there is still no sign of the missing dime. Then put the half dollars in your pocket, leaving people wondering where the dime could be.

One neat touch explains the mystery. Arrange the coins exactly as described, and when ready to drop the lower half dollar, extend the tip of the right second finger (Fig. 2), making the lower half dollar turn over as it drops, letting the dime fall beneath it (Fig. 3). So the dime has vanished!

Then, when you drop the upper half dollar *straight down, without the flip-over,* they will be absolutely baffled. That's when you can drop all three coins—two big half dollars and the little hidden dime—into your left coat pocket and let people argue where the dime went.

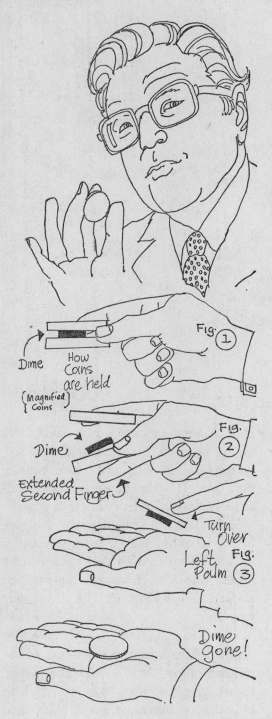

Dime

How Coins are held

(Magnified) Coins

Fig. 1

Dime

Extended Second Finger

Fig. 2

Turn Over

Left Palm

Fig. 3

Dime gone!

BUDDHA MONEY MYSTERY

Half a century ago, this effect was highly popular. Today it is almost forgotten and is therefore more baffling than ever. It is also easy to make as well as to perform. So here is how it goes:

Show four squares of paper, ranging in size from 8½ inches down to about 6 inches, all creased so that each can be folded into a neat square, the smallest about 2 inches (Fig. 1). The sheets may vary in color as well as size—for example, you can use red, brown, green, or yellow. Place a coin in the center of the smallest sheet—No. 4—fold the paper, turn it over, and place it in No. 3, which in turn is folded, turned over, and placed into No. 2, which is also folded, turned over, and placed in No. 1 (Fig. 2).

Now comes the magic: Fold the large sheet—No. 1—then tap it a few times, whisper a mystic word, and unfold it. Follow that by unfolding Nos. 2, 3, and finally 4, which all prove to be completely empty; the coin has vanished! Show both sides of Sheet No. 4; then go through the folding process exactly as before. Again, the mystic word; and when you unfold the sheets, the coin has returned!

It all depends on Sheet No. 2, which actually consists of two identical squares pasted back to back. This should be done carefully, so that the creases come together exactly when both squares are folded (Fig. 3). A dark paper—such as brown, purple, or black—should be used, so there will be

Duplicate pasted on back

Fold each sheet & turn over

Double your money!

Wow!

less chance of anyone noting that the folded square is double. Inside the bottom No. 2 sheet is a duplicate of No. 3; inside that, a duplicate of No. 4.

When the coin is placed in No. 4 and the sheets are folded and turned over as described, the hidden section of No. 2 comes uppermost. So when you unfold it, you automatically switch the duplicates of Nos. 3 and 4 for the originals. When sheets 3 and 4 are opened, the coin is gone. To bring the coin back, you merely reverse the procedure. When the sheets are unfolded (as in Fig. 1), you can pick them up in a group and shake them, convincing people that the coin has really vanished.

In unfolding the sheets, a clever touch is to give No. 4—the innermost sheet—to the person who placed the coin therein, so that he or she can later claim that the vanish or transformation took place in his or her own hands. This also distracts attention from Sheet No. 2, which is the real clue to the mystery.

VARIATION: Instead of vanishing a coin, you can change a half dollar into two quarters; or a quarter into two dimes and a nickel. Similarly, a U.S. coin can be changed into a Canadian coin of the same denomination, or any other transformation that you want.

The more freely the sheets are handled, the better. They can even be turned over while unfolded, with the exception of No. 2, which can be turned over casually along with No. 1.

FIND THE COIN

For this trick you need four coins, all alike in value—say, nickels, dimes, or quarters—but three are United States coins and one is a Canadian coin. You also have four sheets of paper, each about six inches square, and the coins are placed in separate sheets, which are then folded into smaller squares that look exactly alike (Fig. 1).

The folded papers are then mixed and given to you. Holding them in your left hand, you draw them off one by one with your right and press each paper to your forehead to get the "vibration" (Fig. 2). Finally you announce which paper contains the Canadian coin, and when the paper is unfolded, your guess proves to be correct. Only it isn't just a guess, because you can hit it correctly every time you try.

The secret is a tiny bar magnet, which you hold in the bend of your left fingers. Place the mixed papers over it and draw them out, one by one, starting from the bottom and replacing them on top (Fig. 3). The Canadian coin is magnetic, but U.S. coins aren't, so when you feel the magnet grip a paper, you will know that you have the Canadian coin. At the finish, take all the coins from the papers and drop the papers in your pocket, letting the magnet go with them. If you want, you can use some extra papers and let people put in any coins—U.S. or Canadian—yet you can always tell which is which.

NOTE: A good plan is to have a set of four ordinary papers folded together, like the special packet used for the Buddha Money Mystery (page 120). After doing one trick, you can fold the papers all together and put them away. Then later bring out the other packet to show a different trick.

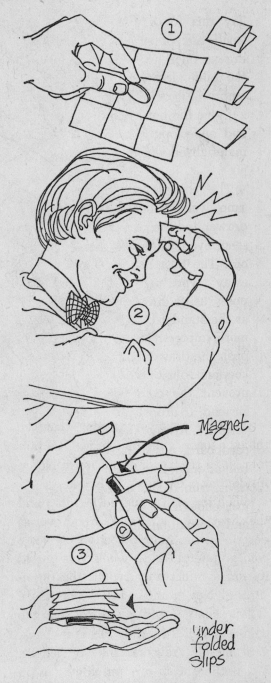

Try this for a real surprise! Show a small box of safety matches with its drawer open and shake the matches on the table, leaving the drawer entirely empty (Fig. 1). Close the drawer (Fig. 2), give the box another shake, open it, and out plops a half dollar, magically materialized within the matchbox! (Fig. 3).

The coin is actually there all the time, wedged between one end of the drawer and the cover, where it lurks unseen, even when the drawer is pushed out. The best box to use is the "giveaway" type, used for advertising purposes, as its drawer is only half as deep as the standard, so the half dollar looks more impressive when it appears. Just push the drawer shut with your fingers, keeping your thumb at the other end to prevent the coin from coming along. Instead, it drops into the drawer.

NOTE: Always use a box made of cardboard, *not* wood, as the cardboard bulges enough to wedge the coin. If too tight, trim the inner end of the drawer just enough to accommodate the coin and you will be all set for the trick.

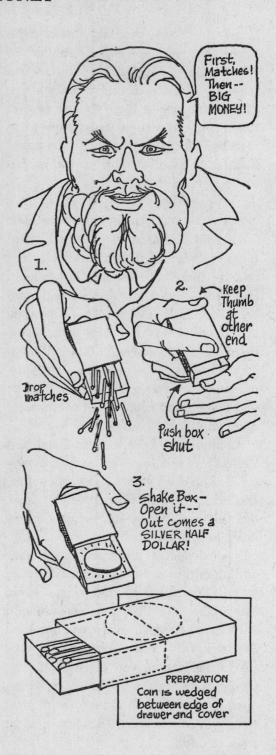

First, Matches! Then-- BIG MONEY!

1. Drop matches

2. Keep Thumb at other end
Push box shut

3. Shake Box- Open it -- Out comes a SILVER HALF DOLLAR!

PREPARATION
Coin is wedged between edge of drawer and cover

ODDS AND EVENS

Here are three puzzling tricks with coins that are somewhat similar in effect, but decidedly different in method. This means that when you are asked to do one of these tricks a second time, you can switch to another trick, thereby baffling your friends even more. Each trick involves small coins, as follows:

QUICK CHANGE Have a person take some coins from his pocket and count them, without telling you how many he has. He then holds them in either hand and concentrates on whether the number of coins is odd or even. You then take some coins of your own, place them in one hand, and state: "Whichever you have, odd or even, I'm going to change it. If your coins are odd, mine will make them even; if yours are even, mine will make them odd!"

Assume that he opens his hand and shows seven coins. You say: "Seven—odd"; then open your hand to show five, and add: "And mine make eight, nine, ten, eleven, twelve—changing *odd* to *even*, as I said I would!"

It all depends on the simple rule that adding odd to even brings an odd total; while odd added to odd brings even. Just make sure that you have an odd number of coins—in this case, five—and the trick will work either way. If your friend had shown you eight coins, you would have said: "Eight—even," then opened your hand, adding, "and nine, ten, eleven, twelve, thirteen change even to odd!"

Done emphatically, the trick can be repeated, as most people will be too surprised to realize that they fell for such a simple rule of arithmetic.

LEFT AND RIGHT Have someone take odd number of coins in one hand, an even number in the other, without stating which is which. Tell him to multiply his left-hand coins by 2, those in his right by 3, then add the two results. That done, he names the total aloud. After deep concentration, you announce which hand holds the even number of coins and which hand holds the odd number.

The total tells you all you need, so you really don't have to concentrate. If *even*, the right-hand coins are *even*; if *odd*, the right-hand coins are *odd*. *Examples:* Left, 7 coins. Right, 6 coins. $7 \times 2 = 14$; $6 \times 3 = 18$; $14 + 18 = 32$, an *even total*. Left coins odd; right coins *even*. *In contrast:* Left, 4 coins. Right, 9 coins. $4 \times 2 = 8$; $9 \times 3 = 27$; $8 + 27 = 35$, an *odd total*. Left coins even; right coins *odd*.

ADD THEM UP Show some loose coins in each hand, then close your fists and state: "In one hand, I have coins that add up to an *odd* total; in the other hand they add up to an *even* total. Try to guess where the *odd* total lies, but whichever hand you pick, you will be wrong!"

Suppose your friend points to your left hand. Open it and lay down a dime, three nickels, and three pennies, counting them: "Ten, five, five, five, one, one, one—twenty-eight cents, an *even* total, so you lose." Then, to prove you won legitimately, you open your right hand and count its coins—a dime, two nickels, and five pennies: "Ten, five, five, one, one, one, one, one—twenty-five cents, an *odd* total"—as you said it would be.

This raises one question:

What if your friend had pointed to your right hand instead of your left, when picking the hand with the odd total? The answer is quite simple. In that case, you count the coins one by one, without referring to their values: "One, two, three, four, five, six, seven, eight, an *even* number"—in your right hand; and "One, two, three, four, five, six, seven, an *odd* number"—in your left hand. So they still add up in your favor.

THE DOUBLING COIN

Show a coin and lay it on the table. Let everyone see that your hand is empty. Pick up the coin, then open your hand. Two coins drop out instead of one. Drop them on the table where they may be examined—a quick way to double money!

Two coins are needed for the trick. One is placed on the table, the other beneath, held to the under surface of the table by a piece of gum or a dab of soap. In picking up the visible coin, slide it from the table with your thumb. This lets your fingers go beneath the table, where they get the second coin, which appears with the other coin in your hand.

TELL A COIN

Toss three coins on the table and turn your back, telling someone to flip the coins over one by one, saying "Turn" each time he does so. He can turn any coin as often as he wants, but at the finish he is to cover *one* of the three coins with his hand. You then turn around, look at his hand as though you had X-ray vision, and announce "heads" or "tails." Whichever the case, when he raises his hand, everyone sees that you are right. To prove that it isn't just guesswork on your part, you can repeat the test as often as you want; and always you will be right.

The secret is to note all three coins at the start, to see if "heads" are "odd" or "even." One or three heads count as *odd*; none or two represent *even*. If heads are odd to start, you keep thinking "odd" until the person says "Turn" as he turns over a coin; then you switch to "even"; then back to "odd" on his next announcement of "Turn"; and so on, to the finish. Conversely, if heads are even to start, you begin by thinking "even" and keep switching to "odd" and back to "even."

Regardless of which coins are turned, if you finish on "odd," the heads will still be odd; on "even" they will still be even. So by simply noting the two coins still in sight, you know exactly what the hidden coin must be. If you end on "odd," and heads are *even* (none or two), the hidden coin is a head; while if an *odd* head shows, the hidden coin must be a tail. If you end on "even," an *even* number of heads proves that the hidden coin is a tail; whereas an *odd* head means that the hidden coin is also a tail.

INSTANT COIN VANISH

Spread a handkerchief on a table with its far corner pointing away from you and lay a large coin a trifle to the left of the center (Fig. 1). Fold the near corner up to the far corner, forming a triangle and covering the coin (Fig. 2). Next, fold the right corner at the base of the triangle over to the corner at the left (Fig. 3). For a final fold, bring the top corner of the triangle down to the left, stopping a little short of the lower left corner (Fig. 4). Then roll the right edge of the triangle down to the lower left (Fig. 5), leaving the lower left corner still in view. All is so simple and aboveboard that trickery seems impossible as you prepare for the sudden climax.

Pick up the left corner of the handkerchief and you will find that it consists of two layers, one above the other, forming a double corner. Take the upper corner with your right thumb and fingers; the lower corner with your left thumb and fingers (Fig. 6). Lift the corners, and in the same action pull them rapidly apart to the full extent of the handkerchief (Fig. 7). If you do this properly and swiftly, you will find to your own amazement that the coin has vanished!

Actually, the coin is still there, lodged in a deep crease running diagonally from corner to corner, but the effect is so startling and convincing that no one realizes it!

To conclude the trick, raise both hands, bringing them together, and take both ends of the handkerchief in the left hand. Slide the right hand beneath, so the left hand can lower the center into the right palm. You then bundle the handkerchief with the right fingers and put it in your pocket, the coin going with it.

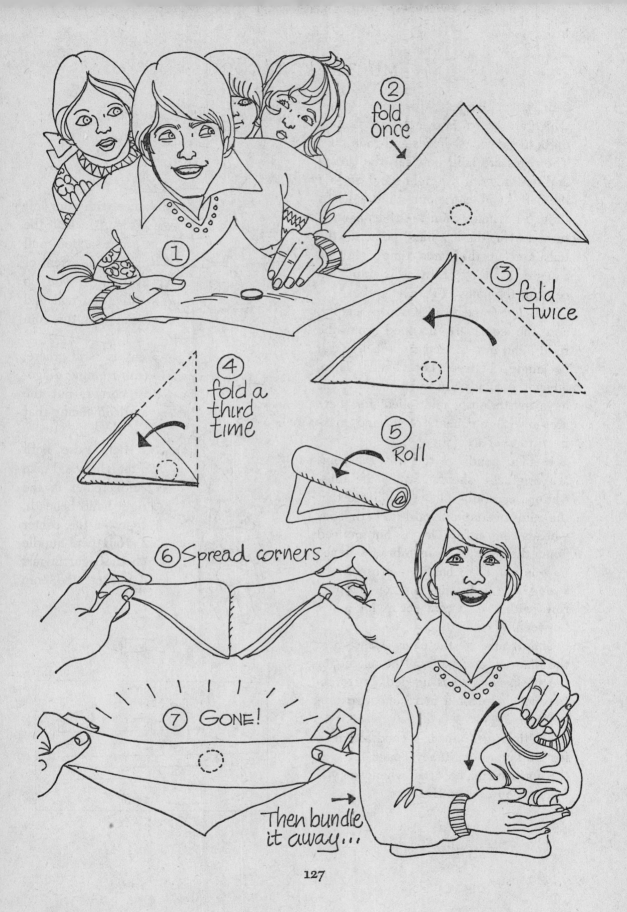

② fold once

①

③ fold twice

④ fold a third time

⑤ Roll

⑥ Spread corners

⑦ GONE!

Then bundle it away...

MULTIPLYING COINS

This effect begins with three coins, which are shown in overlapping fashion on both sides, first heads and then tails. The coins are held between the thumb and forefinger of the right hand, so that the left hand can point to the heads (Fig. 1). Then, when the right hand is turned over, the left hand points to the tails and at the same time everyone can see that the right hand is empty except for the coins (Fig. 2).

The left hand is also shown empty, and the coins are dropped from the right hand into the left so that they can be jangled between both hands. Then, when the hands are opened, the coins have mysteriously multiplied, for there are now three coins in each hand, making a total of six! (Fig. 3).

It all depends on the way the coins are originally shown. Study the illustrations carefully and you will see that the coins overlap outward on both sides —heads and tails. This is not noticed when the coins are shown briefly, hence no one suspects that they are actually seeing five coins in two overlapping rows with a sixth coin occupying a slot between.

Simply arrange the coins as shown in the diagram and you will be all set for the trick. No skill is needed, but practice will help for a more effective presentation.

Multiplying Coins is a good alternate for Double Your Money (page 116), as the former can be used whenever you have time to set up the coins.

How Coins Are Held

COIN ON FOREHEAD

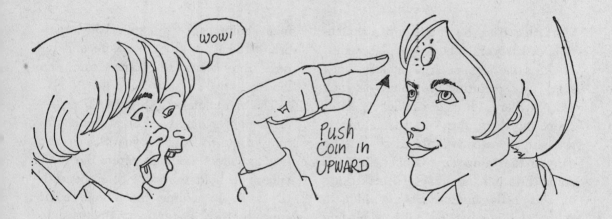

This is one of those puzzling little stunts that appear to be really magical when presented in an offhand manner.

Borrowing a small coin, set it against the center of your forehead. The coin apparently becomes magnetized because it adheres there.

Even though you tilt your head forward and shake it from side to side, the coin does not fall. Finally remove the coin and return it to its owner.

It all depends on the way you put the coin in place. Set it against your forehead and push the coin upward. This creates suction and the coin will stick firmly after you take your hand away from it.

DOUBLING MONEY

Hold 3 coins UNDER tray, 3 coins over...

Start this trick by taking up a collection. Ask several people to place coins of the same size—such as nickels—on a small tray, counting the money as they place it there. Three are sufficient. After collecting them, turn to a spectator and ask him to extend his hand so that he can be the temporary banker. Let the coins slide into his hand. To make sure of this little investment ask him to count the number of coins, replacing them on the tray one by one.

To his amazement, the holder of the coins discovers that he has twice as many coins as he thought. You appropriate the coins from nowhere and return the borrowed coins from the lenders.

The extra coins—in this case, nickels—are actually yours because at the beginning of the trick, when you pick up the tray to collect the money from the audience, you hold the extra coins beneath the tray. In sliding the visible coins from the tray, let the hidden coins slide from beneath. All go into the hands of the spectator.

COIN IN HANDKERCHIEF

A handkerchief is stretched cattycornered between the hands; a knot is tied in the middle. Then give the handkerchief to another person and ask him to untie the knot. Amazingly, a coin is found inside the knot.

To accomplish this, hold the coin hidden in the fold at one corner of the handkerchief. Twirl the handkerchief toward your body, jump-rope fashion. Do this loosely so it forms a hidden tube allowing you to let the coin slide down to the center. Now tie a knot in the center, keeping the hidden coin inside the knot, and you are all set for the finish.

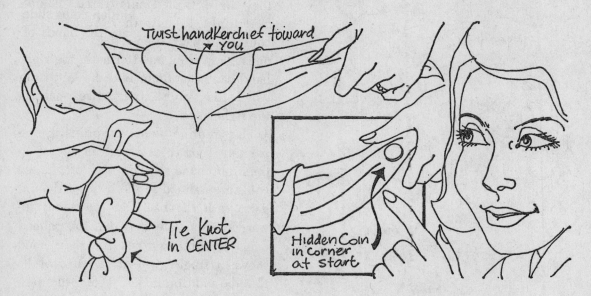

Twist handkerchief toward you

Tie Knot in CENTER

Hidden Coin in corner at start

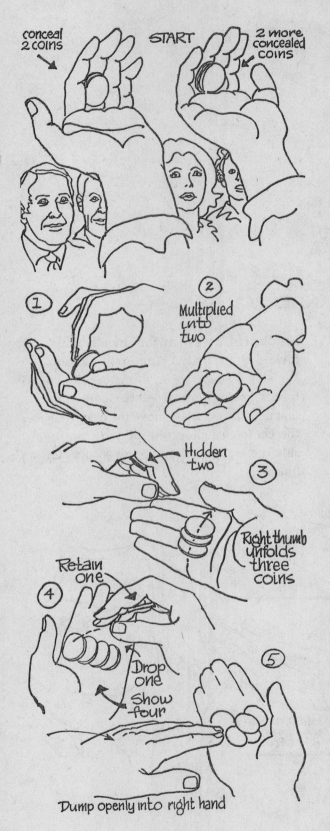

conceal 2 coins

START

2 more concealed coins

①

② Multiplied into two

Hidden two

③ Right thumb unfolds three coins

Retain one

④ Drop one Show four

⑤

Dump openly into right hand

ONE TO FIVE

This is a quickie among coin tricks—one of those surprises so easy to perform that it will catch the average spectator totally off guard. With one surprise following another in quick succession, the trick builds to a climax that makes it an excellent adjunct to a more ambitious coin routine.

A half dollar is held in the tips of the right thumb and forefinger, and promptly dropped into the cupped left hand. The performer blows on his left hand, opens it palm upward, and shows that the coin has doubled into two. The left hand dumps the two coins into the right, palm upward, and shows that they have tripled into three. Poured from right to left, they become four coins; and back from left to right, they finish as five. As an aftermath, the right hand can pour them into the left, from which they vanish, only to reappear in the right hand.

This routine depends primarily on palming four coins in advance—two in the right hand, two in the left. These coins are palmed in the bend of the fingers, with the backs of the hands toward the spectators, so that the palmed coins are unseen when the right hand shows a single coin at the tips of its thumb and forefinger. From the performer's view, as shown in START position, it will be noted that not only are

132

the coins neatly concealed; in addition, each pair can be kept closely together by clamping their edges firmly with the fingers, so that when shown openly later, each pair will appear to be a single coin.

Working from that basis, you begin by showing the single coin (Fig. 1) and insert it in the left hand, which is already partially cupped to receive it. With your left thumb, press the single coin against the two coins in the bend of the left fingers, blow on the left hand, tilt it forward, and show that the coin has apparently multiplied into two (Fig. 2).

What people actually see is the single coin overlapping the palmed pair, which also looks like a single coin when viewed from above, provided that you keep the pair neatly nestled in the finger bend. Bring your hands together, remarking that you will put the "two" coins in your right hand, but simply thumb the single coin from your left hand so it drops into the bend of your right fingers as you turn the right hand palm upward.

Since the single coin drops on the pair already clamped in the bend of the right fingers, you still apparently have just two coins, but as you spread them with your right thumb (Fig. 3), the "two" prove to be three. In doing this, the left fingers retain their original pair,

so you remark that you will toss the three coins back into the left hand and see what happens next. Here, you push out two of the right-hand coins, letting them fall into the bend of the left fingers, while retaining the third coin in the right finger bend (Fig. 4). All in the same action, the left thumb spreads the two coins with the pair already there, showing four in the wide-open left hand.

These are dumped openly into the right hand, joining the coin still palmed there, so the left hand can conclude the process by spreading all five coins upon the outstretched right palm (Fig. 5). Done in rhythmic fashion, the routine has a cumulative effect, with the coins increasing one by one, just rapidly enough to keep you nicely ahead of the spectators. After the first move, the rest are done more and more openly, giving the final impression that the hands were shown empty at the start.

For the aftermath, the left hand can overlap the five coins neatly on the right palm; then, turning to the left, the right hand lets the coins slide into the finger bend while pretending to pour them into the open left hand. The coins are then "vanished" from the left hand and can be reproduced singly by the right hand, by pushing them up with the right thumb.

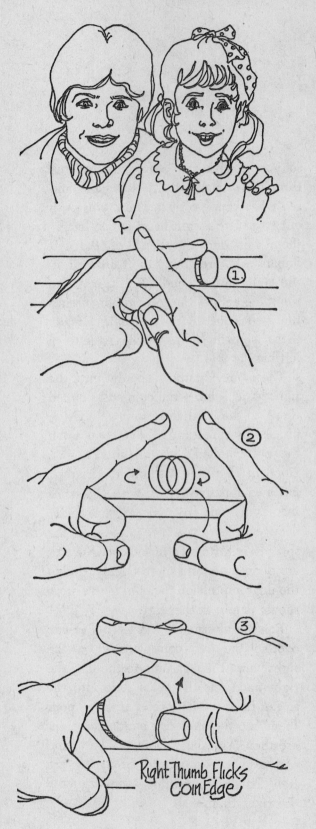

Right Thumb Flicks
Coin Edge

SELF-SPINNING COIN

Although this is a rather trifling trick in itself, it can be built into a real "wow" when you get half a dozen people trying it all at once and have them wondering why they can't do it when it looks so simple when you do it. Here is how it looks:

Set a large coin upright on a smooth-surfaced table, keeping it in position by pressing the tip of your extended left forefinger against the top edge of the coin. Extending the tip of your right forefinger at an angle, begin stroking the left forefinger slowly and steadily from knuckle to tip (Fig. 1).

State that this process will cause the coin to spin, and as you increase the pace, suddenly the coin goes spinning away as you lift your left forefinger (Fig. 2). Naturally, other people want to try it, but they fail dismally, because the coin does a flip-flop just when they think they've reached the final stroke. But for you, it always spins!

The reason is that the finger stroking is purely a bluff. As you keep speeding it (as shown in Figs. 1 and 2), you extend the tip of your right thumb, under cover of your forefinger, just enough to flick the edge of the coin as you go by (Fig. 3). That starts the coin spinning, and no one suspects the real motive power. Don't worry if it does a few flops to start. That only makes it more surprising when it really spins.

134

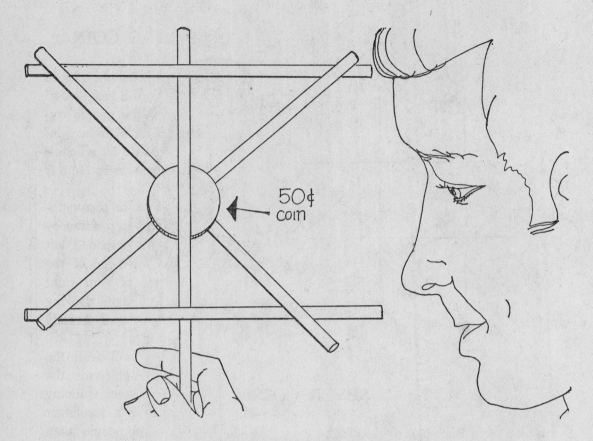

50¢
coin

COIN AND STRAWS

Five drinking straws and a coin are required for this perplexing stunt. The object is to use one straw as the only support by which you will lift the remaining straws and the coin as well. It looks impossible, but it can be accomplished.

Lay one straw on the table; across it place two straws several inches apart.

Cover them with two straws that cross diagonally like a letter X; slide those straws into position by pushing them beneath the original straw. Wedge the coin between the original straw and the center of the X. Lift one end of the first straw and all the articles will come up together.

SEVEN COINS

Draw four cross lines like a Tick-Tack-Toe game on a sheet of paper and connect the diagonal ends. Number the corners from 1 to 8 starting with the topmost left line, then ask for seven coins. The idea is to start each coin at a point and move it straight to another point, leaving it there. Every coin must finally rest on a different point. But you cannot start a new coin from a point already occupied.

You do this perfectly and rapidly, then let others try it. They fail because the trick is a real twister. The trick is to move each new coin to the point from which you started the coin before. Start the first coin anywhere: after that, follow the rule. Example: 1 to 4, 6 to 1, 3 to 6, 8 to 3, 5 to 8, 2 to 5, 7 to 2.

TRICKY TURNOVER

This starts like a "heads and tails" puzzle but winds up with a tricky finish. Arrange six coins in a row, alternating heads and tails, thus:

1	2	3	4	5	6
Head	Tail	Head	Tail	Head	Tail

Now challenge someone to move two coins side by side to a new position; then to repeat the move with another pair of adjacent coins. Only *two* such moves are allowed, yet at the finish there must be three heads together and three tails, with no spaces between.

It sounds impossible, which it is—unless you know the trick. Move coins 2 and 3 to the left end of the row, using both hands; and with your left hand, *turn over* coin 2 (a tail) in a forward direction, putting *three heads* at the left. Now move 5 and 6 into the space vacated by 2 and 3, again *turning over* your left-hand coin, No. 5, converting it from a head to a tail. The row will finally stand:

Head   Head   Head   Tail   Tail   Tail

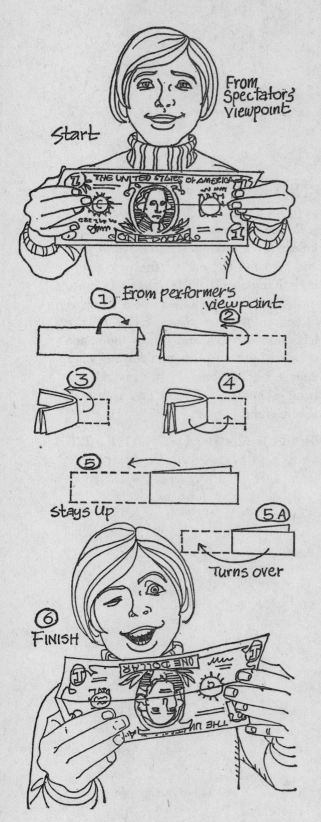

Start

From Spectators' viewpoint

① From performer's viewpoint ②

③ ④

⑤ stays up

⑤A Turns over

⑥ FINISH

FOLD THE BILL

Try this with a dollar bill, holding it in front of you and spreading it out between the thumbs and fingers of each hand so that the portrait of George Washington faces the audience, head up. Then, taking it from *your viewpoint*:

1. Fold the upper half frontward, horizontally.

2. Fold the right half frontward to the left.

3. Again, fold the right half frontward to the left.

4. Unfold the back half (two layers) out to the right.

5. Unfold the front half outward to the left.

6. Bring the front half of bill upward horizontally.

The bill will then be spread exactly as it was originally, and other people, following your folds with bills of their own, should naturally get the same results, until you go through the routine again, and to their surprise the bill finishes upside down. From then on, you can work it time and again, ending it whichever way you want, much to their surprise.

It all depends on one neat, practically undetectable switch. When you come to Step 5, where you unfold the front half outward to the left, substitute 5A by unfolding the *back* half outward to the left. Your left fingers, reaching over to the right, hide the action so naturally that no one will note the difference. The surprise comes when, in Step 6, you bring the front half upward.

COINS THAT STAY

Lay a piece of paper between the top edges of two drinking glasses. Place a coin on each end of the paper to serve as balance weight. The trick is to remove the paper without dislodging either coin. This seems impossible.

There is no problem if you hit the paper squarely in the center, driving directly downward with your forefinger. The blow will prove double-acting. The center of the paper reaches the table so quickly that the ends sweep out from beneath the coins. The coins remain balanced on the tumblers.

strike down on center of paper

FLOATING DOLLARS

Two crisp dollar bills are shown in the right hand, each with its portrait side upward. The right hand slides the uppermost bill onto the outstretched thumb and fingers of the left hand, which is held palm upward; then lays the other bill crossways on top. As the right hand makes magnetic passes above the bills, they float slowly and mysteriously upward until they are suspended in midair, three inches above the left palm (Fig. 1).

To prove that there is no "gimmick," the right hand lifts the upper bill and slides it beneath the lower bill, which continues to float alone (Fig. 2). The right hand leaves it there and makes more passes, causing the floating bill to descend slowly and settle on the bill in the left palm. The right hand gathers the two bills, squaring them together, then shows them on both sides and puts

them away, leaving onlookers wondering whether or not the whole thing could have happened.

It can happen and there is a "gimmick" to it, despite the "proof" that there is none. The gimmick is a strip of flexible, transparent plastic, measuring 5 by 1½ inches. This is attached lengthwise to the back of a dollar bill, with a square of double-sided Scotch tape, or some other suitable adhesive, at the very center. This gimmicked bill is placed squarely on top of an ordinary bill, with portraits upward, so that both sides can be shown with the plastic hidden between.

The right hand slides the gimmicked bill onto the outspread left hand, portrait upward, so that the tips of the left thumb and little finger can press the ends of the plastic strip, after the ordinary bill has been placed across the gimmicked bill. Slow, steady pressure causes the plastic to hump up in the center, automatically elevating the crossed bills (Fig. 3). Viewed from above, the floating dollars hide the plastic completely (as in Fig. 1), and being transparent, it will remain unseen even from a slight angle. In its arched position, the gimmick allows space for insertion of the ordinary bill (as in Fig. 2), perplexing observers all the more.

By gradually releasing pressure with the left thumb and little finger, the gimmicked bill descends in the same mysterious fashion and the right hand then turns it so that it covers the ordinary bill. Since the plastic is again hidden between the bills, they can be turned over together without revealing it and pocketed or replaced in an envelope or wallet, to conclude the mystery.

Pliable Plastic Strip (Narrower than bills)

141

COINS FROM STRING

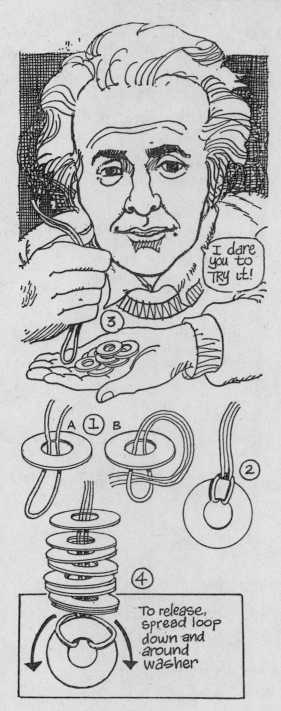

I dare you to TRY it!

A ① B

②

③

④

To release, spread loop down and around washer

This was originally performed with Chinese coins, which accounts for the title; but it can be worked just as easily with metal washers, sold at hardware stores for a few cents each. Using a thin string about two feet long, bring the ends together and push them through the hole in the center of the washer; then push the ends through the loop that you have formed (Fig. 1).

Draw the ends tight, so that the washer is firmly attached to the loop (Fig. 2). Thread the remaining washers —half a dozen in all—onto the ends of the string, so that when they slide down, they will be blocked by the bottom washer. Give the ends of the string to a spectator to hold and cover the washers with a handkerchief. Reaching beneath the cloth for a few moments, tell the person to pull the ends of the string, and when you whisk away the cloth, there are the washers lying free in your other hand! (Fig. 3).

It's all really done at the very start, which is why it is so deceptive. When you loop the washer on the string, it becomes fixed (as shown in Figs. 1 and 2), but all you have to do to release it is to spread the loop at the top and work it down and around the sides until it reaches the bottom (Fig. 4). When your helper pulls the ends of the string, the loop will run right through the hole, and as the bottom washer falls, the rest will go with it!

CHAPTER EIGHT: Tricks with Cards

Cardini

AMONG THE MASTERS of "manipulative magic," the career of Cardini stands unique. Some flashed to fame in meteoric fashion, only to fade when interest in their type of work died out. Others switched to some specialized branch of magic, like Houdini, who dropped his billing of the "King of Cards" to become the acknowledged "Handcuff King." A few curtailed their manipulative efforts to move into bigger fields, most notably Thurston, who started as a "Card King" and wound up with a full evening show. Even those who continued as manipulators often completely changed their style, hoping to keep up with the times.

This did not apply to Cardini. Once he had established his act, Cardini stayed so far ahead of the times that his imitators didn't catch up with him for a period of nearly fifty years.

Cardini's specialty, as his stage name implied, was card manipulation. Under his real name of Richard Pitchford, he was working behind a counter in Gamage's department store in London, at the start of World War I. Between customers, he practiced catching cards at his fingertips and spreading fans of cards. One day Max Malini, a performer noted for his close-up card tricks, came by and shook his head at the amateur. "Forget that card flipping," Malini told young Dick. "You'll never get anywhere with that old stuff!"

Dick had to forget his card flipping temporarily when he joined the British Army, but when his outfit was assigned to the trenches, he began to break the monotony as he had at Gamage's. His fellow soldiers liked the way he plucked cards from the air and fanned them,

and when cold weather numbed his hands, he began wearing gloves while doing his routine, with some success. He also developed sleights using lighted cigarettes, which were about the only other items available in the trenches. Wounded in action, Dick was transferred to a hospital where they supplied him with cards and gloves to continue his practice.

After the war, Dick worked up a magic act that included some of his manipulations, but a scarcity of bookings made him wonder whether Malini might have been right. At intervals, Dick returned to his old job at Gamage's, where he continued to improve his sleights until they became the dominant feature of his act. When he came to the United States in 1926, as "Cardini," he had developed his card and cigarette routines to such near perfection that he dropped everything else.

Cardini's act had become a prestidigitatorial pantomime, a serio-comic expression of artistic dexterity that was unrivaled by anyone.

Attired in evening clothes, with white gloves, black cape, and top hat, he made the perfect man-about-town as he strolled unsteadily on-stage, where a pageboy—a part played by his wife, Swan—relieved him of a newspaper he was trying to read, so that he could take off his gloves. Even that gave him trouble when a fan of cards appeared in his gloved right hand; and in puzzled fashion, he produced fan after fan, dropping all of them in the outspread newspaper, which the pageboy unfolded to receive them.

Finally disposing of his gloves, Cardini produced cards singly with his bare hand and would top it off when a lighted cigarette appeared at the tips of his fingers. As he started to smoke the cigarette, he caught another with his other hand; then both his hands were producing cigarettes alternately and throwing them into a receptacle that the pageboy supplied. Then Cardini became more bewildered than ever and other surprises followed: bits of byplay with lighted matches, the sudden appearance of a billiard ball, which changed color when Cardini tossed it in the air, and finally the appearance of a lighted meerschaum pipe, which he smoked as he bowed off, to thunderous applause.

Cardini's music was highly appropriate, beginning with the dreamy strains of the classic "Zenda Waltz" that Thurston had used during his card manipulations, and ending with the popular "Smoke Gets in Your Eyes" as his cigarette productions neared their peak. Naturally, his act underwent some changes, as did the places where he appeared, which ranged from the Palace Theater, where he first appeared on Broadway, to the Radio City Music Hall, which was opened five years later, and finally Manhattan's larger hotels and nightclubs.

"Imagine my act in a big place like the Music Hall!" Cardini once quipped. "Why, the people in the top balcony were so far away, they must have thought I was the Dancing Handkerchief in person!"

Actually, though, they recognized him as the one and only Cardini, the proof being that he was constantly wanted for return engagements at that greatest of all variety halls. Cardini faced a real problem, however, during the cigarette shortage of World War II, since he threw away dozens of partly smoked cigarettes in the course of his act. He treated that humorously, too, when he told his friends: "Any time you see people getting excited over my act, don't let them throw money on the stage. Just tell them to throw me cigarettes."

During that period, I saw Cardini often between shows at the Biltmore Hotel, where he was playing an extended engagement. I was editing *The Conjurors' Magazine* for the Magicians' Guild, which had elected Cardini president; and together we went over sleights and tricks, picking those with intriguing twists that would be suitable for publication. Cardini came up with this neat version of the Four-ace Trick that dated back to his days at Gamage's and is as good now as it was then:

From the top of a pack, you deal the four aces in a face-up row: clubs, diamonds, spades, hearts. Then turn them face downward and deal three face-down cards on each ace. One packet—say, the one with the ace of spades—is chosen by the spectator, so you gather the other three and add them to the pack, which is then thoroughly shuffled, the three odd aces with it. You then snap the pack three times—once for each ace—and slowly riffle the outer end of the pack, card by card.

As people watch the cards fall, they find that the three aces have gone. You can repeat the riffle to convince them of that fact; then, as final proof, you have someone turn up the packet containing the chosen ace of spades. With it are the other three aces!

Amazing indeed, yet quite simple when you know the secret. From a duplicate pack, take three aces—clubs, diamonds, hearts—and using scissors cut them a trifle shorter than the other cards. These are the three aces that you have on top of the pack to start, along with the ordinary ace of spades, which should be third from the top. Under that, have six different cards; then the three regular aces.

Deal the top four cards in a face-up row; all aces. Turn them face down and deal three cards on each, putting the normal aces all together in an "ace packet." Tell a spectator to point to any two packets in the row. If one happens to be the ace packet, you pick up the other two and lay them aside. If neither is the ace packet, you pick them up just the same and lay them aside. Either way, two packets remain on the board, one being the ace packet.

Now you say: "Pick up either packet that you want." If he picks up the ace packet, you simply pick up the other packet and lay it aside with the first pair, leaving him holding the ace packet. If he should pick up the other packet, tell him to lay it aside with the first pair, which leaves the ace packet on the board. Either way, you clinch his "choice" by picking up the three packets that were laid aside, adding them to the pack and giving it a thorough shuffle.

You then snap the pack three times and riffle the far end slowly and repeatedly, letting people watch for the aces. Having been cut short, each ace falls along with the card ahead, so naturally they have vanished, only to show up in the "chosen" packet, along with the ace of spades. These are replaced on the pack, which can then be put away in the card case to conclude the Four-ace Trick.

A SPECIAL NOTE ABOUT
CARD TRICKS

Tricks with cards fall into a class of their own. It is actually quite easy to present a complete magic act using cards alone. You would have the choice of two types of programs: (1) card tricks performed while seated at a table; and (2) those performed while standing before a group of people, where you can move from one person to another. Here are some suggestions for creating an act that should flow smoothly and gain the attention of your audience.

For a table routine, a good opening effect is:

Count Along or Perfection Prediction: Since this depends on a special arrangement of the cards, it is preferable to "set up" your own pack beforehand, unless you have time to arrange a borrowed pack. Otherwise, proceed with your next trick:

Cops and Robbers: In going through the pack to pick out three jacks and a king, you can easily place others on top or bottom, as required. Follow with:

Twenty Cards or New Deal Twenty-card Trick: Either of these similar tricks is good at this spot, the New Deal being preferable for keener spectators.

Sense of Touch: Specially effective, since it can be worked beneath the table, this trick can also be repeated, dependent upon reactions of spectators.

Crossed Colors: Excellent at this point in the program, as you can lower your hands as if to do another trick beneath the table, secretly leaving a few cards in your lap as you change your mind. This gives you the needed setup.

Quick Poker Deal or Super Poker Deal or both: With a few comments on the game of poker, you can easily arrange the cards while looking through the pack. However, if the audience is not really interested in poker, it may be preferable to finish with a repeat of Crossed Colors. Then, by having another pack in readiness, you can bring it out for an encore:

Cardini's Ace Trick or Perfection Prediction: Either of these is a standout in its own right. If desired, Perfection Prediction can be used as an opener instead of Count Along, as PP also depends on a specially arranged pack.

For a group routine, you can put on more of a show, getting away from tricks involving deals, and giving preference to tricks that look better at a fairly long range. By having a table or chair handy, you can lay aside required items, such as some extra cards, a handkerchief, a glass, or a setup pack.

An excellent opener for this type of program is:

The Riffle Pack: Have your pack set up for Lost and Found. After doing the trick, with two spectators, run through the pack and set it up for:

The Magic Ace: Here you show the fan of three cards to one spectator after another, giving each a brief look before you proceed. After that:

The New Magic Ace can be shown as a follow-up. By laying the pack on table or chair, you can pick up the glass and handkerchief, show them, and make ready for:

The Amazing Card Vanish: After vanishing the card from the glass, lay glass and handkerchief aside, put the pack in its case, and drop it in your pocket, as though concluding your performance. Then, as an afterthought, pick up another pack from the table and present, as an optional effect:

The Jumping Card: This requires special cards, which is why you have the other pack ready. After The Jumping Card, lay its pack aside and bring the pack from your pocket, in order to proceed with:

The Baffled Burglars or The Modern Burglars: Either of these is easily set up while looking through the pack for certain cards; and the cards, when fanned, can be shown very effectively to person after person. This leads up to a climax with:

Steal the Sheep: A story with a surprise ending, which will top off your program.

VARIATION: Instead of The Jumping Card, you can use Slide-away Card, which involves a few special cards from a pack that is lying handy. By eliminating The Jumping Card you can use The Rising Card as an encore.

Also NOTE: When placing the original pack in your pocket, you can put the rubber band around it and later bring out a duplicate pack, all set for Instant Reverso, or another "riffle" trick, which you can perform before The Baffled Burglars.

There are many tricks to choose from. Once you've practiced them you can pick and choose which ones work best for you. You can even improvise on the tricks. Remember: Have fun!

Basic Riffle Arrangement
(alternately LONG & SHORT)

①

② Keep cards in position with Thick Rubber Band

③ Backs with white margins

EVENS END

ODDS END

TRICKS WITH THE RIFFLE PACK

The "riffle pack" is a term applied to a pack that has been specially arranged so that certain cards will appear or vanish when the end of the pack is riffled. This means that you must first learn how to riffle the cards, which is really quite easy. Place the pack face down across the palm of one of your hands, gripping it with the fingers. Press the thumb of your other hand against the inner end of the pack and with the fin-

gers, bend up the outer end of the pack.

By gradually releasing the cards with the fingers, they will spring forward in rapid succession, revealing the faces one by one as they are turned toward a spectator. By arranging or "setting up" the pack beforehand, the riffle can be used to produce some surprising magical effects, as follows:

Deal a fifty-two-card pack into two

face-down heaps. From those heaps, take cards in order: left, right, left, right, and so on, placing each card face down on the one before, but placing those from the left an inch or so forward, those from the right an inch or more back (Fig. 1). That done, square the pack neatly, preferably by tapping it on the table; then carefully press the sections closer together, until less than one-quarter inch protrudes at each end. By using a pack that has backs with white margins—which are necessary in some tricks—you can measure this exactly, by bringing the end of each "short" card up to the margin of the design on the "long" card just beneath it. Place a joker on the bottom of the pack, then put a fairly tight, thick rubber band around the center to keep the cards in position, and your riffle pack will be ready for business (Fig. 2).

By holding the pack face frontward in the left hand and riffling the upper end with the right fingers, only the faces of the projecting odd cards will show, as if they were really "long" cards. By turning the pack around and riffling the other end in the same manner, the projecting even cards, become the equivalent of "long" cards, showing an entirely different array of faces (Fig. 3). Thus you are working with two sets of "long" cards until you remove the rubber band and press the ends of the pack squarely together.

After that, you simply have an ordinary pack. So any tricks done with the riffle pack must be the opening part of your program and cannot be repeated, unless you bring out another pack later.

Different tricks depend upon different setups, as shown on the following pages:

LOST AND FOUND

In this effect, you riffle a pack of cards and tell a spectator to pick any card he sees there. Then ask him to name the card aloud—say, the jack of spades—but when you riffle through the pack, you tell him he must be wrong because the card is not there. Let him have a look himself when you repeat the riffle and he is forced to admit that his card is gone. So you let him pick and name another—say, the ten of hearts—but when you riffle the pack again, it disappears, and the jack of spades, which he called out, returns.

All this depends on the riffle pack in its simplest form. Deal the two heaps in any order and assemble the cards alternately, as described, using a joker on the front, with a rubber band around the pack. Riffle the top end, letting the spectator remember any card he sees. Lower the pack, bring the other end up, and riffle that end, telling him to look

for his card. Naturally, the card is gone, since you are now riffling the other set of twenty-six. If he thinks of a new card, you can vanish it and at the same time bring back the old one by simply inverting the pack again and riffling the upper end.

In each case, the spectator thinks that he is seeing all fifty-two cards, as will the rest of the audience. As you proceed with the trick, you can remove the rubber band and keep the pack firmly clamped in your left hand each time you invert the pack.

For the finish, relax pressure and riffle the pack sharply so that the ends come even; then spread the pack face up between your hands and pick out the chosen cards as you come to them, proving that all are really in the pack. Once you've closed the pack you can proceed with various effects requiring an ordinary pack.

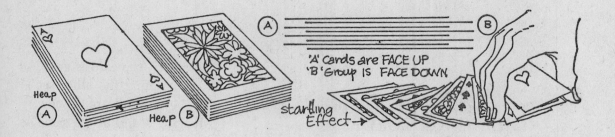

'A' Cards are FACE UP
'B' Group IS FACE DOWN

Heap A

Heap B

startling Effect →

INSTANT REVERSO

In this application of the riffle-pack principle, you first riffle the cards to show the faces; then turn the pack around and show the backs in the same fashion, calling attention to their color or making some remark about their design. Repeat this process so that everyone sees that the pack is quite normal, and continue with a few such riffles after you have removed the rubber band. Then:

Giving the pack a sharp riffle or a quick slap, you spread it face up between your hands, and to everyone's surprise, half of the cards have turned face down, so that they run alternately face up, face down, throughout the entire pack. Weeding out the "facedowners" as you go along, you finally turn them face up and add them to the rest of the pack so you can proceed with other tricks requiring an ordinary pack.

Set up the pack by dealing two heaps as already described, but keep the heap at the left (the A cards) face up and turn the heap at the right (the B cards) face down. Deal the face-down cards forward, the face-up cards farther back,

so that each type is sandwiched between the other. In this case, the joker is added to the top of the pack, face down, or you can simply discard the final face-upper so that the top, or rear card of the upright pack will be face down.

With the two types of cards pressed neatly in position, the pack is held upright, with or without the girding rubber band, and the cards are riffled face-front by the right fingers, apparently showing the faces of all fifty-two cards, although people only see half that many. The pack is then deliberately turned around, so the upper end can again be riffled, this time showing the backs of what is supposedly the entire pack. This should be repeated for the benefit of all observers, to emphasize the normal condition of the pack.

The pack is then lowered and either snapped or slapped; the cards are turned face up and spread wide, showing every other card face down, a truly magical effect. Or the pack can be spread in ribbon fashion, endwise along the table, producing the same startling effect.

CHANGING COLORS

For a fast surprise, this rates among the best. The pack is shown with the joker at the front and slowly riffled to show that it consists entirely of black cards. After everyone is convinced of that fact, you blow on the pack, riffle it again, and every card has changed to red. Another blow, another riffle, and the blacks are back again. To conclude the effect, the pack is turned face down, snapped, turned face up, and spread. Now all the cards run alternately red and black.

To set this up, sort the pack into reds and blacks, lay each group face up, and gather them in the usual alternating fashion. At the finish, put the joker face up on top so it will become the front card of the pack, and gird a rubber band around the pack. Riffling the top end will show one color; by inverting the pack and riffling the other end, you can show the other. In each case, snapping the pack or slapping it will cover the turn-around.

When the pack is spread to show the alternating colors, few people will realize that they saw only half the cards during each riffle, as they are unaware of the principle involved. This is an excellent preliminary to any trick in which you intend to use a group of red and black cards.

COLOR FANTASY

This elaboration of Changing Colors is actually a double-barreled baffler. You begin by showing a pack with the joker on the front and riffling the cards to show that they are all reds. Then turn the pack around, showing a red-backed card at the top, and riffle the pack again to show that the backs are all red. That process can be repeated, as you emphasize, "A pack of all red cards, with all red backs!"

Now you pick up a joker that is lying on the table and turn it over to show that it has a blue back. Slide this card face down under the rubber band so that it becomes the top card of the face-down pack. Turning the pack face-front, snap it and say: "Watch! The red cards are now blacks!" When you riffle the pack, amazed observers see that you are right. All the original hearts and diamonds have now turned to spades and clubs!

To add to the mystery, you remark: "Of course, the blue-backed joker did it all; and look at what it did to the backs, as well!" Turning the pack around, you riffle it, showing that the backs are all blue. Remarking, "Red cards—red backs; black cards, blue backs—let's bring them both together," turn the pack face up and spread it, showing that the faces of the pack are alternately red and black!

But there is still a surprise to come.

Lay the front joker to the left, face up, and separate the alternating colors into two piles, the red cards at the left and the black cards at the right, finally laying the rear joker at the far right face up. You then say: "Remember, the red cards all have red backs, like this joker at the bottom." With that, you turn the first joker face down, showing it's red, and add: "While the black cards all have blue backs, like this joker that you saw me put on top." Here, you turn the second joker face down showing its blue back.

Then pick up the red cards with your left hand and the blue joker with your right. Brushing the face-up reds with the face-down blue, you say: "Look what a little touch of blue can do." Turning the red cards face down, you spread them and show that all their red backs have changed to blue! Then, picking up the black cards, brush them with the face-down red joker, saying, "And a little touch of red does the same thing to those blue backs." Sure enough, the backs are now all red!

Two full packs—one red-backed, the other blue-backed—are needed for this setup, each pack having a joker. Follow the instructions carefully, or you may fool yourself before you even start; the trick is that good. Take all the black cards from the red-backed pack and place them in a face-up heap at the left; then take all the red cards from the blue-backed pack and place them in a face-up heap at the right. Assemble these alternately, left, right, left, right, with the red cards forward, the black cards backward. Square the pack, pressing the ends inward to the riffle position, and put the red-backed joker face up on top, adding the rubber band.

To perform the effect, lay the pack face upward on the left hand, and with the right hand, turn the lower or inner end forward, so the pack is face down. Raising the pack upright, riffle the upper end with the right fingers, showing all red cards. Again turn the lower end upward and forward; then repeat the riffle, showing that the backs are also red. Lower the left hand so that the pack lies flat and turn the pack over sideways, showing that the top card has a red back. Take the blue-backed joker and carefully slide it face down under the rubber band.

Now raise the pack upright with the left hand and riffle it with the right fingers, showing that the faces have all turned black. Turn the entire pack upward and forward so you can riffle it and show that the backs are all blue. Remove the rubber band and turn the pack face downward, spreading it to show alternating reds and blacks, while you lay the jokers aside for the surprise finish as described.

Many card players are intrigued by tales of legendary gamblers who could stack cards during a poker game and deal from the bottom or the middle of the pack as readily as from the top. Since most of these people have no idea of how poker hands can be set up, or how easily some false shuffles can be executed, it is possible to amaze them by catching them unaware, thereby gaining credit for skill that you do not actually possess.

This Quick Poker Deal is a case in point, as it begins with a very emphatic shuffle of the pack, after which you deal five poker hands and turn them up, showing that they are just "run of the mill," which is expected after such a thorough shuffle. You then gather them up in any order that anyone suggests, give the cards a few cuts, and deal another round, to show how futile it all can be—until you turn up the hand that you dealt for yourself.

There, in all its glory, is a royal flush, consisting of an ace, king, queen, jack, and 10, all in the same suit, the highest hand in the entire pack!

Arrange all this beforehand by simply going through the pack as though starting an ordinary trick. During this casual procedure, you weed out the high cards in one suit—say, diamonds—and slide them to the top of the pack. Or, if you prefer, you can have the pack already set with those cards on top; then simply have the pack lying handy.

Either way, you turn the talk to gambling and state that it is difficult indeed to count on getting a good poker hand from a properly shuffled pack. To prove your point, give the pack three or four good shuffles, taking care, however, to hold the top cards to the last, so that your royal flush remains on top. Then follow that with an overhand shuffle, using either the "double pull-off" or the "group shuffle"—or both—again keeping the top five cards intact.

Now comes the fancy part. Deal the cards face down, forming five hands of five cards each, as in poker, and say something like: "How good do you think these hands could be?" Before they can reply, you add: "I will show you how bad they are." Whereupon you turn them up and spread them, showing five terrible hands. Review them aloud for effect: There may be a pair of fives, a hand with a working straight, and so on. Then you suggest that a member of your audience pick up the cards hand by hand, in any order, and let you deal them again.

But no matter how the cards are gathered, every fifth card in the deal will be yours, giving you the royal flush that you set up a long way back.

THE GAMBLER'S DREAM

This deal is a setup from the start. There are no shuffles or cuts, as the convincer in this type of presentation is the fact that after dealing worthless hands, merely gathering up the cards should not be sufficient to suddenly turn them into good hands. Yet that is exactly what happens.

Remarking that good poker hands are hard to come by, deal a round of five hands and turn them up. The result is what you anticipated. The best hand has a pair of 9s, which is still not good enough to open the pot. However, after turning up the hands and pointing out their faults, just gather them up in any order, lay them face down on the pack, and deal another round using a little trickery. Then, turning them up, hand by hand, you comment:

"Now, let's see how the gambler made out. He gave the first player a jack-high straight, good enough to open the pot and maybe good enough to win, but not quite, because the second player has it already beaten with a queen-high flush. Naturally, he boosted the pot, but the third player gave it still another boost when he found himself looking at a full house, with kings up. Still, the next player did better, with four aces, which had everybody beaten, until the gambler showed his hand—a king-high straight flush, the best possible hand in the pack when someone else is holding four aces!"

All this works automatically. To set it up, lay the hand face up but mix each hand individually, so its cards will come out irregularly. Lay hand 4 on hand 5; 3 on 4; 2 on 3; 1 on 2; and turn the whole batch face down on top of the pack. Deal five hands face down and turn them face up from left to right; show they will look worthless, as in the first illustration, though this will vary, according to how each hand was mixed. Gather the hands face up in any order; turn them face down on top of the pack and deal again. That will give you the five "pat hands" that you can spread and display as finally shown.

SUPER POKER DEAL

This is the ultimate form of a repeat poker deal wherein two hands are dealt, and the hand on the left is turned up to show a full house. Then, when gathered just as they are, the dealer continues to show a full house—or certain other combinations—in the hand on the left, culminating with the turnup of both hands, showing four jacks on the left and four aces in the dealer's own hand. This is accompanied throughout by a running story, which will be given in brief, following the explanation of the method.

For the setup, arrange the cards from the top down: red jack, black jack, red jack, odd card, black jack, ace, ace, ace, ace. Pack follows in any order.

Deal the cards face down, alternately left, right, left, right, left, right, left, right, left, *right*. The final card is not actually dealt, but is used to scoop up the face-down heap at the right, thus replacing the entire heap on the pack. The heap at the left is then turned face up and spread sufficiently to show its cards in their exact order. The uppermost card of the face-up group is then used to scoop up the other four cards and replace the pile face down on the pack. That sets the cards for the next deal.

The results at the end of each deal run as follows:

1. Show a full house on left: A, A, J, J, J (scoop with uppermost jack).

2. Show a full house on left: J, A, J, A, J (scoop with uppermost jack).

3. Show four of a kind on left: A, A, A, A, J.

Here, after scooping up the face-down heap on the right and replacing it on the pack, turn up the heap on the left and spread it, but *do not* scoop it up with the jack. Instead, gather it as is and lay it face down on the pack, as though completing the routine.

4. Show two pair on left: J, odd, J, A, A.

Again, after scooping up the face-down heap on the right, and putting it on the pack, turn up the heap on the left, show it, but *do not* scoop it with the uppermost card (an ace). Pick it up as it is and lay it face down on the pack.

5. Show a full house on left: A, J, A, J, J.

Scoop up the face-down heap on the right and replace it; but this time, after turning up the heap on the left and spreading it slightly, scoop it up with the uppermost jack, as with the early deals, and replace the heap face down on the pack.

6. Deal two hands in left, right fashion, but this time complete the deal entirely, dropping the final card on the heap at the right. Show four jacks on the left: odd, J, J, J, J.

Then turn up the hand on the right and show four aces: odd, A, A, A, A.

The story line runs as follows: As a preface, you deal six cards, alternately left and right, remarking: "A young gambler was so clever that he could always deal three jacks to his partner." Scoop up the heap at the right, keeping it face down as you replace it on the

pack. Then scoop up the heap at the left with the uppermost jack and lay it face down on the pack. Repeat this process a few times, continuing:

"He did it time after time, until finally his partner asked him why he didn't deal complete hands of five cards each. The gambler said that would be harder, but he'd try."

Here you go into the numbered routine as described, making the following comments to match each deal:

1. "He gave his partner a full house, jacks over aces, and to prove how good he was, he gathered the cards . . ."

2. "And dealt the very same hand again, three jacks with two aces, another winning combination. While he was gathering those up . . ."

3. "His partner said he'd like to see him deal something better. So this time, the gambler dealt him four aces."

4. "When his partner asked why he didn't deal four of a kind every time, the gambler said he couldn't, because he never knew which to go after, jacks or aces, so sometimes he came up with two of each, which only counted as two pair."

5. "So he preferred to deal the sure way and come up with the good old reliable full house, which couldn't miss."

6. "However, the gambler said he was always ready to take a chance, so if his partner really wanted four of a kind, he would deal them to him." (Make final deal.) "And there they were, four jacks for his partner." (Turn up hand on left.) "But just to show how good he was, the gambler dealt four aces for himself!" (Turn up hand on right for climax.)

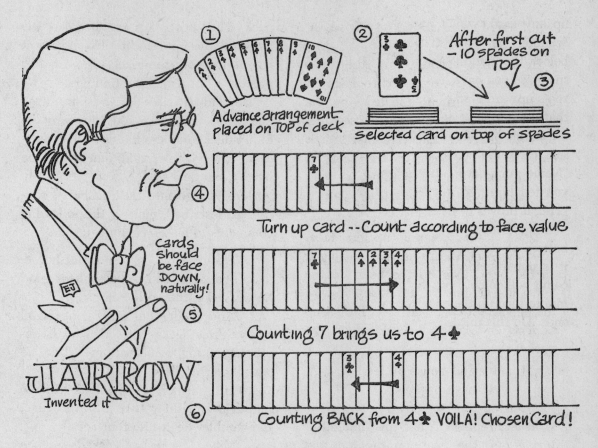

① Advance arrangement placed on TOP of deck

② ③ After first cut — 10 spades on TOP

Selected card on top of spades

④ Turn up card -- Count according to face value

cards should be face DOWN, naturally!

⑤ Counting 7 brings us to 4♣

JARROW
Invented it

⑥ Counting BACK from 4♣ VOILÁ! Chosen Card!

COUNT ALONG

This "find the card" trick can prove to be a real baffler. After a card has been selected and placed back in the pack, the pack is spread face down so the chooser can turn up another card at random and use its spots—say, eight—to count along the row to another card, which is also turned up, so the process can be repeated with its number; and again, with a third card. In the case of a picture card, its name is spelled, letter by letter—as k-i-n-g, q-u-e-e-n, or j-a-c-k.

After a few such counts, you suddenly announce that the next turnup will be the originally chosen card; and it is, even though you yourself had no idea what the original card was!

The trick depends on a setup of the top ten cards of the pack. All are spades, running from ace to 10 (Fig. 1). You can show the remainder of the cards by spreading them face up, but it is advisable to follow with the "group shuffle" to prove that those lower cards are not prearranged. That done, lay the pack face down and invite a person to cut it into two piles, look at the top card of the lower pile, and place it on the upper pile (which has the prearranged spades on top). Then add the lower pile to complete the cut. This buries his chosen card somewhere in the pack (Figs. 2 and 3).

Now spread the pack in a long, overlapping line and tell your helper to turn up any card, which will be used as a "counter" or "speller." If he hits a bit below the middle, he will turn up a spade, so you have him count that many spots upward along the row and stop on that card. Whatever the count—say, six, for the six of spades—it will be the chosen card. So you say, dramatically: "Name your card!" and when he does, you tell him: "Turn it up!" To his surprise, it proves to be his card.

If he turns up a "counter" near the bottom of the pack, the mere fact that it is not a spade will tell you that his count will come short, so you simply tell him to turn up the card where his count ends. Do this until he turns up a spade;

then you know that his next count will hit the chosen card, so you act accordingly.

Should he turn up a "counter" near the top, this situation is still better. You tell him to count or spell downward—that is, to the left—and even if he takes three or four counts to reach a spade, you can still keep cool, for then you say: "It looks like you've been counting in the wrong direction; try it the other way and see what happens." He does, and comes up with his card on the very first try!

After the discovery, a few regular shuffles will mix the spades sufficiently to dispose of any clues to the mystery.

TWENTY CARDS

Most magicians are familiar with this trick in which twenty cards are dealt in face-down pairs, so that various spectators can secretly select a pair. The cards are then dealt in random fashion to form four face-up rows of five cards each, and when a spectator points to the row or rows in which his cards appear, the performer immediately picks out the correct pair.

This century-old baffler was originally styled the Latin Card Trick because it depended on a formula of four Latin words—*mutus, nomen, dedit,* and *cocis*—that served as "keys" to the various pairs, but there are many combinations of English words that will serve

the same purpose. But always, the procedure has been the same—that of dealing the cards in specified positions rather than in regular rows. This, to some observant spectators, may be a clue to the method after they see the trick a few times.

Twenty cards are taken at random, shuffled, and dealt into ten face-down pairs. Two or three persons each pick a pair, turn up the cards, note them, and turn them down again. The pairs are then gathered in any order, so that all twenty cards form a single pile. You begin dealing the cards face up, apparently in hit-or-miss fashion, to form four rows of five cards each. Yet when a person points to the row, or rows, containing his pair, you pick the two cards instantly!

Taking the words "rufus," "steel," "tiara," and "folio" as your keys, you imagine that they are spelled out on the table, in big letters, as follows:

```
R  U  F  U  S
S  T  E  E  L
T  I  A  R  A
F  O  L  I  O
```

In dealing from the pile, place the first two cards on the imaginary R in RUFUS and on the R in TIARA. Put the next two on each U in RUFUS; then two on the F in RUFUS and the F in FOLIO; then S in RUFUS and S in STEEL. Continuing, you place two cards on letters T; two on letters E; two on letters L; two on letters I; two on letters A; and two on letters O.

If a person states that his cards are in rows 2 and 3, you know immediately that they are on T and T; if they are in rows 1 and 4, they are on F and F; if they are both in row 3, they are on A and A; and so on, with all ten pairs.

NEW DEAL
TWENTY-CARD TRICK

Here is a complete switch from the Twenty-card Trick, involving a "new deal" that completely reverses the procedure. Start by dealing ten face-down pairs from a shuffled pack, forming two rows of five pairs each. Spectators note pairs while your back is turned; that done, form your face-up rows of five cards each by drawing at apparent random from the face-down pairs and laying cards in regular order, five to a top row and the same to all successive rows until all twenty cards have been dealt. When a spectator points to the row or rows containing his pair of cards, you immediately pick them out.

A double formula is the key to the trick. In dealing face-down pairs in two rows each, picture the words "magic store" in big, imaginary letters in the upper left corner of the table, thus:

M A G I C
S T O R E

The first pair goes on the letter M, the next on A, the next on G, and so on, in regular order; hence no one suspects any setup. People look at pairs of cards, when your back is turned; then you begin taking cards at random from the laid-out pairs, laying them in regular rows. Here, however, you use another formula for the center of the table, as with the Latin Card Trick, but it is composed of the *same letters* used in the preliminary layout, namely:

A G O R A
M E T E R
S C O T S
G I M I C

From the laid-out pairs, take a card on letter A of MAGIC and use it to start the imaginary word AGORA. Next, take a G from MAGIC and use it as the second letter of AGORA. For the third letter, take an O from STORE and

164

continue with AGORA; then follow with an R and the second A.

Your layouts will then stand:

```
M   *   (G)   I   C
S   T   (O)  (R)  E
```

Parentheses represent single cards at the spots for the letters shown; the asterisk, none. Below, you have:

```
A   G   O   R   A
```

For the second word, METER in the new layout, you draw M from MAGIC; E, then T from METER; and another E and R from METER, so the layouts stand:

```
(M)   *   (G)   I   C
 S   (T)  (O)   *   *
```

Below, you then have:

```
A   G   O   R   A
M   E   T   E   R
```

For the third word, SCOTS, you draw S from STORE, C from MAGIC, and O, T, and the other S from STORE, giving you:

```
(M)   *   (G)   I   (C)
 *    *    *    *    *
```

Below, you then have:

```
A   G   O   R   A
M   E   T   E   R
S   C   O   T   S
```

For the fourth word, GIMIC, you draw the last five cards from the word MAGIC, thus completing the new layout. If a person sees one of his cards in the top row and the other in the third row, they will be the cards represented by the O in AGORA and the O in SCOTS. One in the second, the other in the fourth, will form the M in METER and the M in GIMIC. Both cards in the third row will be each S in SCOTS; and so on.

SENSE OF TOUCH

Suggestibility more than sensitivity is the key to this surprising test. This trick can be repeated frequently with the same result, giving it the mark of authenticity. From a pack of playing cards, deal two batches of cards; then turn one batch face down and the other batch face up. Shuffle the two together, completely intermingling them.

After everybody is satisfied with the shuffle, turn your back and have someone give the packet to you from behind; or if you are seated at a table, you can put your hands beneath the table so that somebody can hand you the packet from the other side. You then state that through your keen sense of touch, you will separate the packet into two groups, with each group containing *exactly the same number* of face-up cards.

This takes a few minutes to accomplish; then you bring your hands into view, each holding a packet. Lay these on the table and ask someone to go through each packet and weed out the face-up cards. Suppose he goes through the first packet and finds exactly six such cards. When he goes through the second packet, he will find six face-uppers there as well, fulfilling your prediction to the letter.

This will work every time you try it if you use the special system that follows:

In dealing off the batches, make sure you have the same number of cards in each; for example, fifteen. Do not mention that, however; just say that you will use two batches of cards. Shuffle them as stated; one batch of fifteen face up and the other fifteen face down. When you receive them behind your back or under the table count off fifteen cards from your left hand to your right, giving you half the cards in each hand. Have your helper count the number of face-up cards in the right-hand packet.

Let's say there are six; that means the left-hand packet will now contain nine face-up cards and six face down. While everyone is counting the number of face-up cards in your right hand, simply turn the packet in your left hand over, so that those six cards are now face up, equaling the total of the face-uppers in the right-hand packet.

Bring out the packets, let people go through them and find that you are right. If you want to try it again, go right ahead, but it is better to use a new number instead of fifteen so that no one will catch on.

PERFECTION PREDICTION

For a perfect prediction, this rates tops. Take a pack of cards from its case and lay it face down; then write a prediction on a slip of paper, fold it, and place it in the card case. Next, spread the pack with its faces toward you, remove the joker, and divide the pack into two equal heaps. These you shuffle together, face down.

You then turn the pack face up and deal the cards singly into two heaps, red and black, calling attention to the fact that you are taking them exactly as they come from the shuffled pack. Both heaps are turned face down, and a spectator is given the choice of "red" or "black." Assuming he takes the reds, you tell him to cut that heap at any place he wants and take the cards just below and just above the cut, adding their values.

Here specify that an ace counts as 1; the spot cards run in value up to 10; the jack, 11; the queen, 12; the king, 13. Also emphasize that the total of the red pair might be any number from 2 to 26; and whatever it is, count down that many in the black heap and turn up the final card.

Let's say that the spectator's cut produces the 10 of diamonds below and the 4 of hearts above (Fig. 1). Taking the face-down black heap, deal off a total of fourteen cards (ten plus four) and turn up the fifteenth card, which proves to be the jack of clubs (Fig. 2). When someone opens the card case and brings out your prediction, it bears the name jack of clubs.

This baffling effect depends upon a special arrangement of the pack. Take the red cards and set them in numerical order: A, K, 2, Q, 3, J, 4, 10, 5, 9, 6, 8, 7, 7, 8, 6, 9, 5, 10, 4, J, 3, Q, 2, K, A.

On that face-up group, place the joker (or jokers, if the pack contains two); and beneath that, set the black cards, in any order, but make note of the *fifteenth card*, reading from the bottom up, which in this case is the *jack of clubs*, representing your prediction-to-be (Fig. 3).

Bring the pack from the case and lay it face down while you write your prediction (jack of clubs) and place it in the empty case. Pick up the pack and spread it face toward you while you remove the joker and lay it aside, face up. This enables you to cut the pack in the exact center, turning the halves face down, reds in one hand, blacks in the other. Here you state that you will

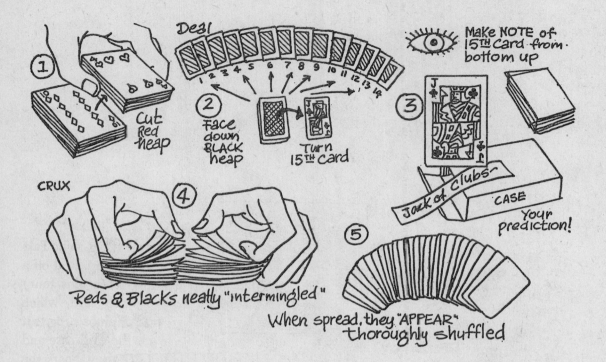

CRUX

Reds & Blacks neatly "intermingled"

When spread, they "APPEAR" thoroughly shuffled

give the pack a "thorough shuffle" that will "completely mix the cards."

Riffle the ends of the packets together slowly, carefully and emphatically, as this is the crux of the trick. You really *are* mixing the cards, and the more neatly you do it, the more thoroughly the reds and blacks will be intermingled (Fig. 4). When you turn the pack face up, and spread it, everyone will agree that it has been thoroughly shuffled (Fig. 5). But when you deal the face-up piles, separating reds and blacks exactly as they come along, the red cards will be in their original setup and the predicted jack of clubs will be No. 15 from the top of the black heap when it is turned face down, because you reversed the order of the blacks when dealing them singly in a face-up heap.

In giving a spectator choice of either heap if he takes the "reds," you say:

"Very well, I want you to cut the heap anywhere and add the spots on two cards that are together, to give us a total from two to twenty-six, which we will count down in the black heap." If he takes the "blacks," you say: "Very well, there are twenty-six cards in your heap. I want you to cut the other heap and add the spots on the two cards that you find there, so we can count down to that number in your heap."

So it works out the same either way; and always, the two red cards where the person cuts will total either fourteen or fifteen. If fourteen, you deal off that many and say: "There is your number, *fourteen;* and that brings us to *your card,*" turning up the fifteenth. If fifteen, you simply deal that many and turn up the final card on the count of fifteen. Then let the spectator bring the prediction from the card case for the climax.

Fig. labels:
① TWO ODD CARDS hidden behind 2nd King

A.
King at Top
King ⎱ in reality ⎱ Inserted
King ⎰ ODD CARDS ⎰ in the middle
King at bottom (in reality 3 Kings)
B. cut

② "Burglars" appear in the middle of the "House"

THE BAFFLED BURGLARS

Though more than one hundred years old, this still rates as a good basic trick, specially for beginners, which is why it has lasted through so many generations. The four kings are taken from the pack and shown in a wide fan, between the thumb and fingers of the right hand (Fig. 1). The left hand helps close the fan and the kings are placed face down on top of the pack, which is also face down.

Stating that the pack represents a house and that the kings are burglars about to rob it, you take the top card, casually show its face, and move it face down to the bottom of the pack, saying: "This burglar went in the front door." Taking the next card, you push it face down into the pack, near the bottom, saying: "This one went in the side door." You then push the next card face down into the pack near the top, saying: "This one went down the chimney." Turning up the next card, you show it briefly, then turn it face down on the pack, adding: "And this one went in the back door."

Here, you cut the pack by lifting off the top half and dropping the bottom half on it, to signify that the burglars are moving about. Then, turning the pack face up, spread the pack on the table, saying: "And when the police arrived, they rounded up the burglars all together in the middle of the house!" There are the four kings, assembled as stated, despite the fact that you separated them earlier (Fig. 2).

The neat factor in this trick is that it is really accomplished beforehand. In bringing the four kings from the pack and arranging them in a fan, you secretly slide two odd cards behind the second king from the left—in this case, the king of hearts. Keep it well squared with the two odd cards behind it when you show the fan and remark "four kings," without calling attention to their order.

Close the fan, go through the routine exactly as described, and the trick will work automatically. The two "kings" that are supposedly pushed into the pack are actually the two odd cards, so they should be kept face down during that procedure, but the faces of the other two can be shown. There are actually three kings on top and one on the bottom when you cut the pack, so that action brings them all together in the center.

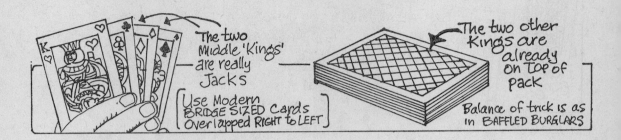

The two Middle 'Kings' are really Jacks

[Use Modern BRIDGE SIZED cards Overlapped RIGHT to LEFT]

The two other Kings are already on top of pack

Balance of trick is as in BAFFLED BURGLARS

Here is the very latest version of The Baffled Burglars in which the century-old effect takes on a new life that will baffle even the bafflers. As in the original, the four kings are shown fanwise in the right hand, but the fan overlaps from right to left, instead of from left to right (Fig. 1).

This enables you to tap the cards with the left forefinger, moving from right to left, while you call off the big spots in the upper right corners: "hearts, clubs, diamonds, spades."

The fan is closed, the packet is turned face down, and the kings are dealt singly on the pack while you again call off the suits in their exact order: "hearts, clubs, diamonds, spades," emphasizing the fact that "there are just four cards—all kings." The top king is moved to the bottom of the pack; the next two are pushed into the pack at intervals; and the final king is shown and left on top. Yet when the pack is cut, turned face upward, and spread, the four kings are found together in the center (Fig. 2).

For this effect, you need a pack of modern bridge-sized cards instead of the wider poker pack. In most bridge packs, the jacks have their large spots in the *upper right corner,* instead of the upper left, or index corner. This enables you to form a reverse fan that looks like four kings, but that actually has two jacks in the middle. These can be spread to show about half of each jack, with the king of hearts spread still farther to the right to show its index along with the big spot at that corner (as in Fig. 1). The real kings of clubs and diamonds are placed on top of the pack beforehand, so after the jacks are "buried" and the pack is cut, all four kings arrive together (as in Fig. 2).

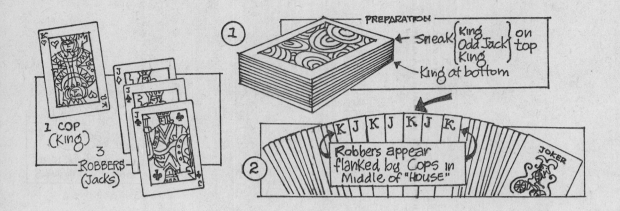

PREPARATION

Sneak {King
Odd Jack
King} on top

King at bottom

1 COP
(King)

3
ROBBERS
(Jacks)

①

② K J K J K J K

Robbers appear
flanked by Cops in
Middle of "House"

JOKER

COPS AND ROBBERS

In this elaboration of The Baffled Burglars, a king, representing a policeman, is taken from the pack and laid face up on the table, along with three jacks, which stand for robbers. The pack is placed face down to serve as a house (Fig. 1). The robbers are turned face down and one goes in the front door, being placed beneath the pack; another, in the window, being pushed into the pack below the center; and the third goes in the back door, on top of the pack. The king is then placed face down on top, to represent the policeman following the last robber into the house.

The pack is cut and the lower half placed on the upper, indicating the robbers moving about inside the house. During that action, you remark that three more policemen are lying in wait to capture the intruders and have already done their job. Turning the pack face up, it is spread to show the four kings in the center, a surprise in itself; but to everyone's greater amazement, the three jacks are there as well, each being flanked by a pair of kings, proving that the officers have taken the robbers into custody (Fig. 2).

The result depends on the subtle introduction of the *fourth* jack in place of one of the original three. While going through the pack and taking out a king and three jacks, you move another king to the bottom and slide two more to the top, putting the odd jack between them. The pack is laid face down in that condition; and from there on, you simply place the three robbers and the lone policeman exactly as described. A cut of the pack brings the whole group to the center, and in the surprise of seeing all those kings, no one will realize that there is a new face among the three jacks.

CROSSED COLORS

Here is a simple yet subtle experiment that shows the power of suggestion at its baffling best. The only requirement is a pack of playing cards, with which you can literally cause people to fool themselves under your artful persuasion.

Start by shuffling the pack, then turn the cards face up in pairs, to see if you can match them. Two red cards go in one face-up pile, while two blacks go in another. Pairs that fail to match are put in a face-down discard pile.

Continue to do this with a dozen cards or more to show how impossible it is to tell what may happen with a well-shuffled pack. You may turn up four red pairs, with only one black pair, and the rest are unmatched.

Having proven your point conclusively, state that you will predict the unpredictable. Have a spectator shuffle the pack while you write something on a slip of paper, which you fold and place in open view. The person then goes through the pack just as you did, setting aside any reds or blacks that come in pairs and discarding all that fail to match. When he is done, tell him to read the slip of paper and then count the red and black heaps for himself.

The slip states: "You will have six more red cards than black cards." When he counts the cards he matched, it proves to be exactly right. If he has sixteen red cards, he will have only ten blacks. Or he might have just ten red cards, but in that case he would have only four blacks. Whatever the proportions, the prediction will be fulfilled.

As already stated, suggestion is the key to this puzzling test. In your pre-

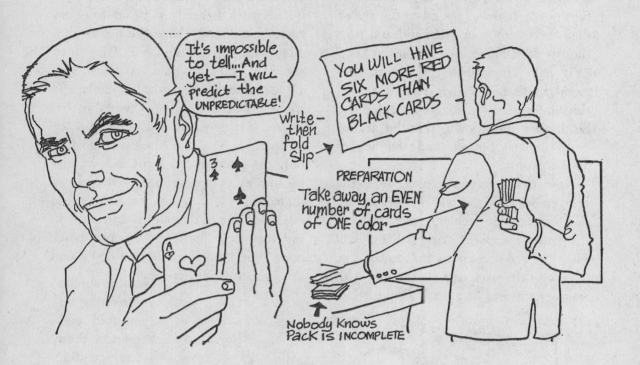

liminary demonstration, you convince people that the pairs of reds and blacks will come out unevenly, which they will, when only part of the pack is used. But with the whole pack, they will normally even up—as fourteen reds and fourteen blacks—because the unmatched cards cancel each other out, something that people overlook because you have talked them into focusing their minds on reds and blacks.

Since people already think that one color is due to predominate, you can make it so by fixing the pack beforehand. All you do is take away an *even*

number of cards of *one color*—in this case, *six blacks*—and put them in your pocket. That means that there will invariably be six more reds than blacks no matter how the cards are paired, because the blacks are already six cards short. So all you have to do is write your prediction and sit back with a wise look on your face.

If you want to repeat the baffling feat, you can add the six blacks and take away some reds—say, four. Your next prediction will then be: "You will have four more black cards than red cards."

175

THE MAGIC ACES

For this baffler, show three aces in a fan —clubs, diamonds, spades—with the ace of diamonds in the center, behind the two black aces. Set the remaining pack aside (Fig. 1). Turning the three cards face down, openly take away the ace of diamonds with your left hand and turn the two black aces face up on the table (Fig. 2). Then push the ace of diamonds, still face down, somewhere in the center of the pack; and turning the black aces face down, put the ace of clubs on the bottom and the ace of spades on top.

Now that everyone knows how the aces stand, take the ace of spades from the top, turn it face up, and thrust it deep into the pack, stating that it will force the ace of diamonds up to the top. Then tap the pack or riffle the end with your fingers and turn up the top card. It proves to be the ace of diamonds, magically propelled up through the pack! As an aftermath, if skeptics insist on looking through the pack, they will find no other ace of diamonds there.

This trick is really done at the very start. You already have the ace of diamonds on top of the pack. The three aces that you show in a fan (as in Fig. 1) are actually the aces of clubs and spades, with the ace of hearts in between; but you neatly arrange the ace of hearts behind the black aces so that only the point of the heart is seen, giving the exact appearance of the ace of diamonds (Fig. 3). After calling the card the "ace of diamonds" and remarking that it is "between the two black aces," you turn the fan face down and do the routine as described.

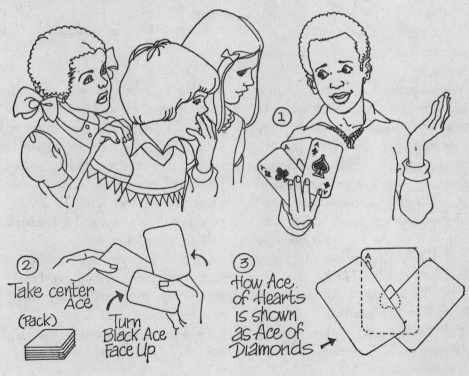

② Take center Ace
(Pack)
Turn Black Ace Face Up

③ How Ace of Hearts is shown as Ace of Diamonds

THE NEW MAGIC ACES

A good follow-up to The Magic Aces, this is also effective when shown independently. Where the original effect is automatic, the new version depends on a timely bit of skill, though not too difficult for anyone past the beginner stage.

Show a fan of three aces—clubs, diamonds, spades—with the ace of diamonds behind and between the two blacks (Fig. 1). The fan is held in the right hand, fingers in front, thumb in back. Tip the fan forward and downward, saying you will take the face-down ace of diamonds from between the other two (Fig. 2). The others are laid face down on the table.

Taking the pack, push the face-down ace of diamonds into the center; then place the face-down ace of clubs on top; show the ace of spades and put it on the bottom (Fig. 3).

Tapping the pack, you magically bring the ace of diamonds to the top, showing it face up; then you turn the pack face up to show that the ace of clubs has gone to the middle in place of it—a most remarkable transposition!

It is all done in the handling of the fan (starting as shown in Fig. 1). Have the ace of clubs overlap the ace of spades and spread the fan wide enough to show that the center card is really the ace of diamonds. Close the fan slightly with the left hand and tilt it downward with your right. As you do this, slide the back card to the right with your right thumb (Fig. 4).

This puts the ace of clubs in the middle instead of the ace of diamonds (as shown in Fig. 2). So each passes as the other when they are put in the pack, enabling them to change places magically, at your command.

177

GRIP A FEW TOP CARDS

THE BALANCED PACK

With your left hand, set the edge of a pack of cards on the outstretched fingertips of your right hand and the pack remains balanced there, while the left hand hovers above, as though steadying it through some magnetic power (Fig. 1). The left hand then takes the pack and offers it to the audience for inspection.

In starting the trick, hold the pack face down in your left hand and push a few top cards toward the right with your left thumb. These cards are secretly gripped between the middle knuckles of the right hand, which is held in a loose fist with the thumb upward (Fig. 2). Now turn your left side toward the audience, straighten the right fingertips, and set the pack edgewise on them, so that it rests against the cards gripped by your knuckles (Fig. 3).

From the front, the entire pack appears to be balanced on your fingertips, but a side view shows how the hidden cards support it, like an easel. Make sure the bottom edge of your support cards do not show below your fingers. At the finish, the left hand swoops down and retrieves the pack, gripping the hidden cards along with the pack itself.

178

SINGLE-CARD BALANCE

This balance of an ordinary playing card is highly effective even at the closest range. All you need to accomplish it is an ordinary pin, with the head gripped between the lower knuckles of the right middle fingers, so that the pin points upward, serving as a prop. The longer it takes to balance the card, the more difficult the trick appears to be, and when you finally lift the card with your left hand, simply spread the right fingers, letting the pin fall unnoticed.

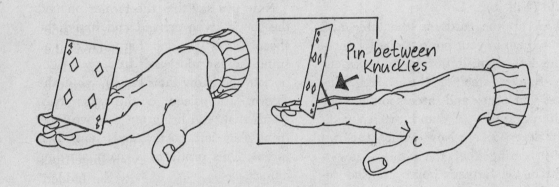

STEAL THE SHEEP

This is an elaboration of the baffler, Thieves and Sheep, performed with paper pellets and described on page 70. This version, which utilizes playing cards, is more suited to a program of party magic because it includes a very clever twist that adds substantially to the mystery.

Seven cards are used: two jacks and five spot cards. Showing the faces of the jacks, place one in each of your pants pockets, stating that the jacks are thieves and that each pocket is a barn where a thief is spending the night. Then state that the spot cards are sheep belonging to a farmer who lives nearby. Then you turn them face down on the table (Fig. 1).

Pick up the cards on the table and place them in your pockets one by one—right, left, right, left, right—to represent the thieves stealing the sheep. This gives you a jack and three spots in your right pocket; a jack and two spots in your left pocket. Now comes the fun part: Stating that the thieves saw a light in the farmer's house, they've decided to put the sheep back to pasture; so you remove the cards from your pockets and place them face down on the table as follows:

From the left pocket, bring out the jack and lay it face down at the left; from the right pocket bring out the jack and place it face down at the left. From then on, draw cards singly from the pockets—left, right, left—placing them face down on the right (Fig. 2). The spectators think that you have simply replaced the five spot cards ("sheep") where they belonged. Instead, you have laid down two jacks ("thieves") at the left and three spots ("sheep") at the right. This leaves two spots in the right pocket.

You then state that when the farmer turned out the lights, the thieves stole the sheep again. So you pick up a card from the right and put it in your right pocket; then one from the left into your left pocket; from right into right pocket; left into left pocket; right into right pocket. This automatically puts five spot cards in the right pocket and two jacks in the left.

Now you say that the farmer phoned the sheriff, who arrived and found the sheep safely in one barn (here you bring the five spot cards from your right pocket and show their faces), while the thieves are asleep in the other barn (with that, you bring out the two jacks from your left pocket and show their faces). This produces a really startling climax.

NOTE: When first putting the spot cards into the pockets, they should be inserted *in back of* the jacks already there. This makes it easy to draw off the jacks instead of spots when bringing the first two cards from the pockets. Also, when drawing actual spot cards from the pockets, their faces can be casually shown before laying them face down on the table.

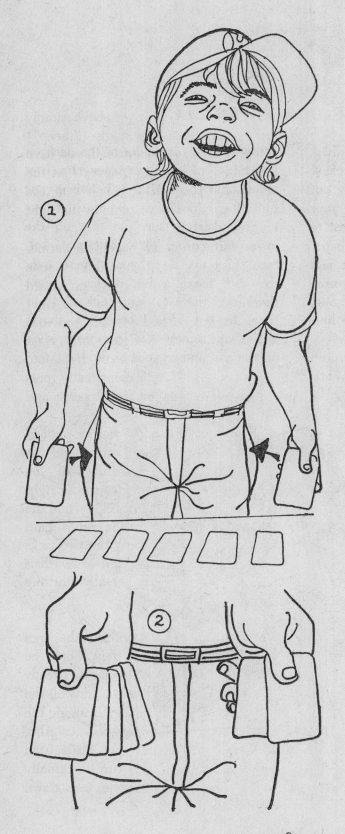

FOUR KINGS IN A PAPER BAG

Start by showing an empty paper bag. Place it on a table. Remove a deck of playing cards from its case. Take out the four kings and show them to your audience. Add the kings to the rest of the cards and put them in the paper bag. Close the bag with a twist and shake it, saying that you are really mixing the cards thoroughly. Open the bag, reach in, and instantly pull out the four kings.

To perform this whiz you must do a little tricky business as follows: When you place the remainder of the deck on the table, pick up a paper clip previously put there. Hide it between your thumb and forefingers. Square the four kings and slyly slip the clip on the lower left corner of the little packet, face sides up. Keep your thumb over the clip, make a fan display, square them, add them to your pack, and put them in the bag. Proceed as above. When you remove the four kings, slide off the clip and leave it in the bag.

Putting Cards in Paper Bag

Removing Cards from Paper Bag

Paper Clip

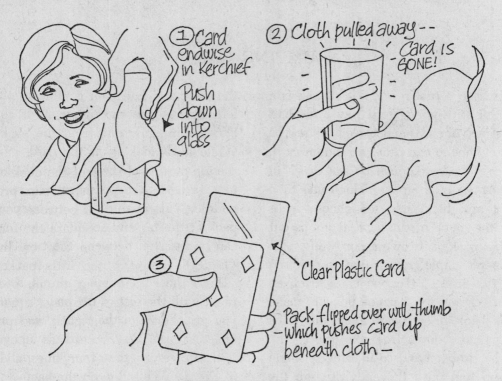

① Card endwise in Kerchief

Push down into glass

② Cloth pulled away -- Card is GONE!

③

Clear Plastic Card

Pack flipped over with thumb — which pushes card up beneath cloth —

AMAZING CARD VANISH

A pack of playing cards, a tall glass with straight sides, and a fairly thick handkerchief are the visible items used in this baffler. To begin, show the pack face down in your left hand and spread the handkerchief over it, stating that you will push the top card up into the handkerchief, which you do. Then have someone grip the end of the card through the cloth and hold it over the glass (Fig. 1).

Next, have the person push the card down into the glass, which you hold, and ask him to guess if the card is red or black. Whichever he chooses, he is wrong, because you promptly whip away the handkerchief and show the glass completely empty. The card has totally vanished! (Fig. 2).

The secret is a piece of pliable plastic, cut to the size of a playing card. Have this on the bottom of the pack, and in covering the pack, secretly turn the pack face up with a forward thrust of the left thumb (Fig. 3). That puts the plastic card on top of the pack so the thumb can push it up beneath the cloth. When your helper takes it (as in Fig. 1), you simply lay the pack face down, take the glass, and whip away the cloth (as in Fig. 2).

Since the plastic card is already invisible, the glass naturally looks empty. By inserting a finger, you can press the unseen card to the side of the glass, in order to show it at closer range to your skeptical audience. In turning away draw out the card, keeping it in the end of your hand, where it will still be invisible while you pick up the handkerchief and casually pocket both together.

This is a particularly good trick for performing at the dinner table. Instead of a handkerchief, a napkin may be used. The invisible card is finally pocketed or simply dropped in the lap.

JUMPING CARD

This trick actually works itself and is a big hit with youngsters. Lay aside half of a pack of cards and spread the rest so that someone can draw a random card. Taking the card, push it face down in the center of the pack, which you then hold upright. When the chooser calls out the name of the card, it jumps out of the pack of its own accord (Fig. 1).

Some simple preparation is required for this trick. Take two cards from an old pack and use a pencil point to make a tiny hole in each card about one third of the way down from the upper end. Cut a rubber band so it forms a single strand and push the ends through the holes. Make small knots on the ends of the rubber bands and fix them in place with mending tape so the cards are linked together (Fig. 2). Place these cards face down at the bottom of the pack with the upper end outward.

In performing, lift off the top half of the pack and lay it on a table to your left. Spread the remaining cards so a person can draw one from the packet. While he is looking at the card, move the top portion of the packet to the bottom, bringing the prepared pair to the middle. This enables you to open the pack at the far end so the chosen card can be inserted between the two cards (Fig. 3).

Push the card home yourself, squaring it with the rest of the packet, which you grip between the right thumb and fingers at the very bottom. When you release pressure, the card will jump (as in Fig. 1). While the chooser is picking up his card, move the bottom portion of the packet-to the top; then turn to the left and drop the packet onto the rest of the pack with your right hand. This enables your left hand to retain the two special cards and drop them in your pocket unseen.

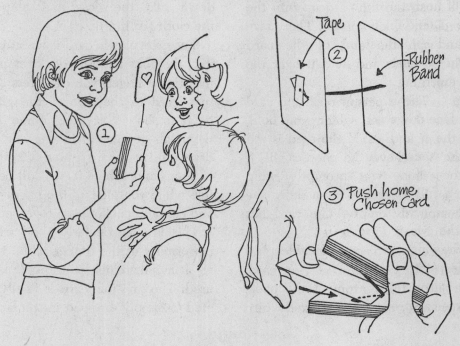

184

SLIDE-AWAY CARD

This neat deception requires two spot cards and a face card—for example, the 10 of hearts, the 3 of diamonds, and the queen of hearts. Holding the cards face up, the 3D and QH are taken in the left hand and spread slightly so that the 10H can be pushed crosswise between them, emerging from the other side (Fig. 1). The 10 of hearts is then turned face down and again pushed between the 3 and the queen in practically the same fashion (Fig. 2). But when the 3 is moved a trifle to the right to give a fuller view of the queen, the face-down card is seen emerging beneath the two red cards, with the left hand drawing it completely clear for all to see (Fig. 3).

This surprising result depends on some special preparation. Take a face card, such as the queen of hearts, and use a sharp blade to cut along the margins on the right side and at the bottom, so that the portrait of the queen is loose on those two sides. This will enable you to push the face-down card through to the back of the queen, when the left fingers press the portrait slightly upward (Fig. 4). That action is covered by the face-up 3 of diamonds (as shown in Fig. 2) so that the face-down 10 of hearts appears to be going *between* the two red cards, as it did before. As the face-down card emerges to the left, draw it clear with the left hand while the right retains the face-up cards, spreading them to show that the face-down card is now below (as in Fig. 3).

TRAVELING CARDS

Take two cards from a pack and show them to your audience. Replace the cards face down in the center of the pack: Strike the pack with your fist, and presto! The cards arrive on the bottom of the pack. This invisible passage is accomplished by the speed of your performance.

Use two pairs of the same cards. The cards you show at the beginning are the 4 of diamonds and the 5 of hearts. On the bottom of the pack you have already placed the other 4 of hearts and 5 of diamonds. Show the first pair quickly. Insert the cards separately and give the pack a magical tap, then show the bottom cards. Invariably they will be mistaken for the pair first shown.

CARD AND PACK

You can discover any card that is taken from a pack of cards and then put back in. Any pack of cards can be used. Ask someone to take a card from the pack. While he shows it to his friends, you hold the pack, giving it a downward bend at both ends. Tell the chooser to replace the card wherever he desires.

You can shuffle the pack provided you do not riffle it. When you deal the cards on the table simply look for one that is straight instead of bent. That will be the selected card.

CHAPTER NINE: A Hatful of Miscellaneous Tricks

The Great Raymond

UNIQUE AMONG THE MEMENTOS of the master magicians is a handsome loving cup, nearly a foot in height, bearing the inscription:

PRESENTED TO

THE GREAT RAYMOND

CHRISTMAS 1912

BY THE COMPANY

That trophy marked a highlight in the career of Maurice Raymond, the international illusionist, who had completed a five-year world tour that August and was traveling eastward across the United States with his full evening show. Although noted for his ability to do a complete performance in half a dozen different languages, Raymond was actually a native of Ohio, and his popularity among his home folks of the Midwest was proven when he reached Chicago, where he filled a series of extended engagements, climaxed during the entire summer of 1913 by an appearance at White City, a famous amusement park.

Traveling eastward, Raymond reached Toronto during October and learned that Howard Thurston, who had succeeded Harry Kellar as America's leading magician, was scheduled to appear in Buffalo. So Raymond made a trip there to see him and found Thurston sitting down to lunch at his hotel with another magician, Eugene Laurant, a top-notcher among Chautauqua performers, who appeared in tent shows during the summer and at concert halls during the winter. Raymond promptly joined them and soon the word spread among the

other diners that three great masters of the magic art were in their midst.

The excitement began after the lunch tab had been paid and the waiter received his tip. Laurant beckoned him back, saying, "You forgot this!" and handed him a coin that proved to be a large Canadian penny of the type then in circulation. Disdainfully, the waiter tossed the copper on the table, where Thurston turned it over, remarking, "Why, it looks like a twenty-dollar gold piece!" It *was* a double eagle, as such coins were then termed, and while the waiter was still staring in disbelief, Raymond picked up the coin and handed it to him, adding, "You had better take it, while you still have the chance!"

Take it, the waiter did, but when he opened his hand to make sure it was still there, he found himself looking at a silver half dollar. Instead of glancing back at the three wizards, he kept right on going, glad that he was getting away with that much money instead of the Canadian penny.

Such were ways and wiles of wizardry, back in the days when people really believed in magic, which some still do, when our present masters of the art get together at conventions not only in America but also throughout the world. But such meetings were rare back then, and after the three wizards parted, they followed different orbits for nearly twenty years. While Thurston was appearing in the larger cities of the United States season after season and Laurant was continuing on Chautauqua circuits that covered the smaller towns, Raymond was increasing his fame as an international illusionist.

In England, Raymond established a workshop where skilled mechanics built new equipment for his frequent tours of European countries, where his remarkable knowledge of the principal languages and various dialects gained him wide acclaim. By 1925, Raymond had another fine, appreciative company, but when he planned another world tour, most of them decided to remain in England, so he had to take on an inexperienced assistant while en route to Brazil. After reaching Argentina, he formed a Spanish-speaking company and for three years traveled northward from southern Chile to Panama, after which he visited the West Indies. He ended his grand tour in Mexico in 1930.

From there, the members of the troupe returned to their respective countries while Raymond continued to California, where he celebrated his own homecoming by presenting a one-hour magical revue during a forty-week tour from coast to coast, with a company of more than twenty persons. Seven curtains rose, revealing an open cabinet, where Raymond appeared from a puff of smoke. Shadows that flitted within a paper-walled box materialized into a living girl, who burst suddenly into view; and later, Raymond produced eight dancers from a larger cabinet that was first shown completely empty.

Other mysteries followed in amazing succession, topped off by Raymond's famous Metempsychosis illusion, in which he and his wife, Litzka, changed places within a locked trunk in less than a split second. Many people remembered this from his tour of nearly twenty years before when they had acclaimed his show as "the best ever" and still agreed that they were right, for along with his full-stage illusions, he presented smaller mysteries that were equally baffling when performed close to the footlights.

One intriguing novelty that Raymond brought from England by way of South America was the trick of tearing two strips of colored tissue paper, crumpling the pieces, and unfolding them fully restored in the form of a Chinese hat, which he placed upon the head of an assistant dressed in an oriental costume. Raymond performed this trick before a special Chinese curtain, with the orchestra playing tinkly music while he unfolded the hat with one hand. So many magicians saw Raymond perform the trick that it rapidly surged to popularity and was extensively copied in simpler form, with an ordinary party hat. Here's how The Paper Hat worked:

Use a green paper hat, with a black band around it. Lay the hat flat and fold it in half crosswise, then lengthwise, and again crosswise, leaving the two ends beneath. Now cut a strip of black tissue paper approximately 20 inches in length and about 7 inches across. Stretch this on a table and apply a dab of paste, or a square of double-sided Scotch tape, about 7½ inches from the left end. Then set the lower end of the folded hat on it, fixing the hat firmly in place. Fold the left end of the strip over to the right and paste it in place beyond the paper hat, thus forming a secret pocket measuring about 5 inches in length, concealing the hat within it.

By pressing this flat, it can be shown as an ordinary strip of black tissue about 15 inches long. Cut another strip of green tissue paper to about the same length and width and have it ready with the prepared black sheet. In performing the trick, pick up the two sheets together and show first one, then the other, turning over the green sheet frequently, while keeping the "pocket" side of the black sheet toward you, so it will not be noticed. Then:

Spread the two strips toward the audience, green in front, and tear off 5 inches from the right end of both sheets. Place these two pieces in front and tear off two more, placing them in front. Now, holding the entire batch between the left thumb and fingers, tear off

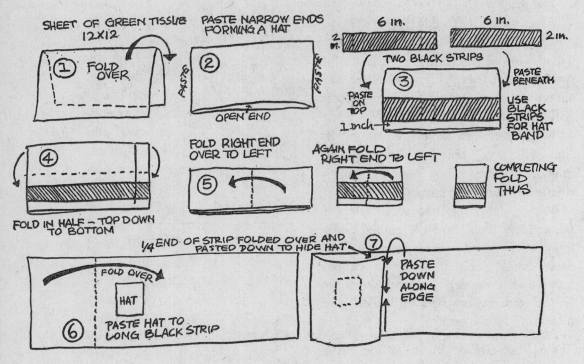

The Paper Hat

the "pocket" at the back with the right hand and place it at the front. This brings the folded hat in sight, but only from your point of view, since no one can see it from the front.

Announce that you will squeeze the torn pieces tightly together, which you do by gripping the folded hat with your right fist, pressing it around the torn pieces, which become firmly wadded. The left hand can help in this process, which seemingly involves the torn pieces only, since no one knows about the paper hat. Then, remarking that you will open the papers and see what has happened, you carefully unfold the paper hat, using both hands—not just one—and spread it for all to see.

The torn pieces are still there, but they are disguised as a tightly wadded pompon, and the spectators, wondering where the party hat could have come from, naturally think that the pompon came along as part of it. After fully opening the hat, you can put it on your head and spread your hands to show them completely empty, finally laying the hat aside and leaving your audience baffled by the mysterious transformation.

191

DICKY BIRDS

This is one of the simplest, easiest, and quickest of tricks. This trick is usually shown to very young children, but it will bewilder those of older age levels as well. Once they have been taught it, they will have great fun showing it to others, making it an excellent introduction to family magic.

Begin by tearing two small slips of paper from the flap of a gummed envelope, sticking one on a finger nail of each hand (Scotch tape or rubber bands also work). Extending those fingers and resting them on the edge of a table (Fig. 1), recite:

"Two little Dicky Birds, sitting on a wall;
One is named Peter, the other is named Paul. . . ."

With that, you dip your right finger beneath the table, saying, "Fly away, Peter," and bring it up again, showing that the paper is gone (Fig. 2). Then, dipping your left finger in the same manner, bring it up, saying, "Fly away, Paul," showing that its paper is gone, too (Fig. 3).

Immediately reverse the moves, dipping the right finger, saying, "Come back, Peter," and then the left, saying, "Come back, Paul," and the bewildered onlookers will see that the paper dicky birds have returned (as in Fig. 1).

It's all done by switching fingers as you go beneath the table. Start with papers on the nails of your second fingers. Bend each finger inward while your hand is momentarily out of sight and extend the forefinger instead, to make the dicky birds vanish. Bend in your forefingers and extend your second fingers to bring the dicky birds back.

Remember: Use fingers that have no rings on them; they will give away the trick!

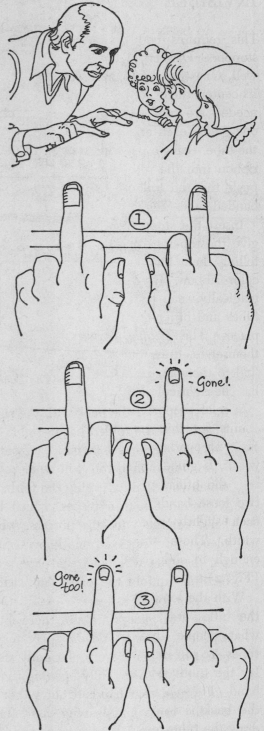

192

INVISIBLE TRANSPOSITION

This requires two plastic tubes with stoppers. Old cigar tubes work very well. One tube has a red band around its center; the other, a green band. Also needed are two ribbons, one red and one green, each about twice as long as the tube. Using a pencil, push the green ribbon into the red-banded tube; then push the red ribbon into the green-banded tube (Fig. 1).

Insert the stoppers in the tubes and give the tubes to two different people, telling them that each has the wrong color ribbon. To rectify the situation magically, snap your fingers toward the tubes and order the ribbons to change places. The people open the tubes themselves, draw out the ribbons, and find to their amazement that each now has the right color!

Special preparation of the tubes accounts for this invisible transposition. First, an overlapping band, one inch in width, is glued around each tube; one red, the other green. You then make two loose bands of those same colors, each slightly more than an inch in width. These should be just large enough to slide over the fixed bands (Fig. 2).

With the loose bands in place, show the tubes and push the ribbons into what people think are the "wrong" tubes. To put the stoppers in place, you lay the tubes side by side in your left hand (Fig. 3). Swing the left hand so the back is toward the audience and draw the tubes upward with your right hand (Fig. 4), retaining the loose bands by pressure of the left thumb. Give each tube to a different person and the

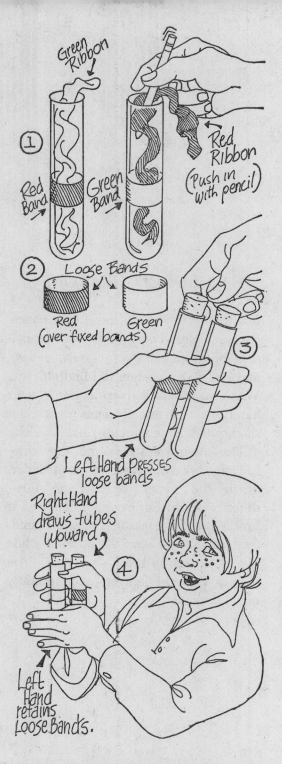

Green Ribbon

Red Band

Green Band

①

Red Ribbon (Push in with pencil)

② Loose Bands

Red (over fixed bands)

Green

③

Left Hand presses loose bands

Right Hand draws tubes upward

④

Left Hand retains loose Bands.

trick is done. The left hand, meanwhile, can pick up the pencil and put it in a pocket, letting the loose bands drop there with it.

COLORED CRAYONS

For this trick you will need four paper-covered colored crayons. Select four colors—for example: black, green, yellow, and red. Ask someone to blindfold you. When one of the crayons is put in your hand you can actually name that color though you are completely blindfolded.

The crayons are prepared very carefully by breaking three of them underneath the paper wrapper in three different spots. For example: The red is broken near the point; the green midway; the yellow near the bottom; while the black has no break—it is solid. You merely feel the crayon and instantly name the color.

COLORED BALLS

Three balls made of different-colored tissue paper are your props for this mental test. Put your hands behind your back and ask somebody to place one of the balls in your right hand. Turn around to face him momentarily and ask him to think of that color so that you can get the telepathic flash. Turn your back to him or her again and name the color.

While you are facing the person, tear off a small piece of the paper ball with your left hand. When you turn your back to him he can see that the ball is really still in one hand, while you can see the color of the torn piece as you bring your left hand around with you on the turn.

THE CLIMBING RING

For this trick you can borrow a ring from someone in the audience to add to the effect, but you should have one of your own in case no other is available. In your pocket, you also have an ordinary pencil fitted with a removable rubber eraser. Holding the pencil upright in your left hand, you drop the ring down over the pencil; then, as you press down on the cap with your right forefinger, the ring begins to climb up the pencil (Fig. 1).

When you lift your forefinger, the ring drops down; but when you apply new pressure, it climbs up toward the cap. This continues until the ring finally reaches the top. Lift the ring off and hand it for inspection; then remove the eraser cap from the pencil and hand them both over for examination as well.

The key to the mystery is a length of thin black thread attached to a button of your coat or shirt. Beforehand, press the free end of the thread against the top of the pencil and fit the eraser cap down over it. Have the thread slack when you drop the ring over the pencil, and when you move the pencil slowly forward, the thread will tighten, causing the ring to climb the pencil (Fig. 2). Pressing the cap is just an excuse for having it on the pencil; and when you remove the cap, the thread drops unnoticed against your body (Fig. 3).

NOTE: A dark shirt or jacket, as well as a dark-colored pencil, are all helpful for this trick!

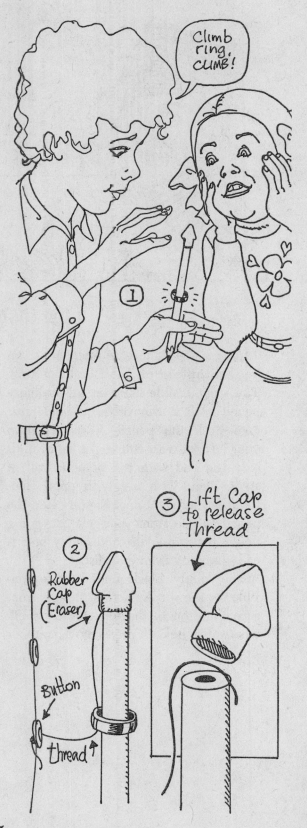

THE RISING PENCIL

This is a good alternate effect that can be used instead of The Climbing Ring. The only visible item is an ordinary pencil with a removable rubber eraser cap. Push the pencil downward into your left fist with your right hand, until only the end with the point is still in sight. Then, with wiggly, hypnotic motions of your right fingers, you cause the pencil to rise from your left fist, going down, then up again, and finally practically jumping from your fist.

The handy black thread is responsible for the spooky action. It runs from a coat button to the top of the pencil, where it is held in place by the rubber eraser cap. In this case, the right hand holds the pencil point upward, then pushes it down into the left fist, so that the thread runs over the left thumb. While the right hand provides finger wiggles to distract attention, the left fist is worked slowly forward or backward, tightening or relaxing the thread, as needed.

A forward thrust of the left hand will provide a final jump as the right hand makes a quick reach to catch the pencil. The cap is then removed so it can be examined with the pencil, as the loose thread falls unnoticed.

THE BOTTLE IMP

For this strange feat of wizardry, you need a small dark bottle and a thin rope about two to three feet in length. Push one end of the rope well down into the bottle and wind the rest of the rope around the bottle itself. Stating that there is an imp inside the bottle, turn the bottle upside down and let the rope unwind. The imp apparently hangs onto his end of the rope, because it dangles from the bottle without falling free (Fig. 1).

To prove that the imp is really hard at work, you take hold of the dangling end of the rope and let the bottle drop instead. The unseen imp hangs on just as strongly, as the bottle now dangles from the rope (Figs. 2 and 3). At the finish, you can draw the rope clear and hand it for examination along with the bottle.

The secret depends upon a tiny ball, preferably of hard rubber and small enough to go easily into the bottle. Have it in the bottle at the start (Fig. 4), and when you wind the rope around the bottle, tilt the neck of the bottle downward (Fig. 5). The ball slides into the neck of the bottle and jams there as you keep drawing on the rope (Fig. 6). As a result, the rope will dangle from the bottle; or the bottle from the rope, as already shown.

By holding the neck of the bottle in your left hand and pulling out the rope with your right, the ball will come along and drop unnoticed into your left hand (Fig. 7). Instead of a rubber ball, you can make one of tinfoil, which works just as well. Make it the right size by adding more foil as needed.

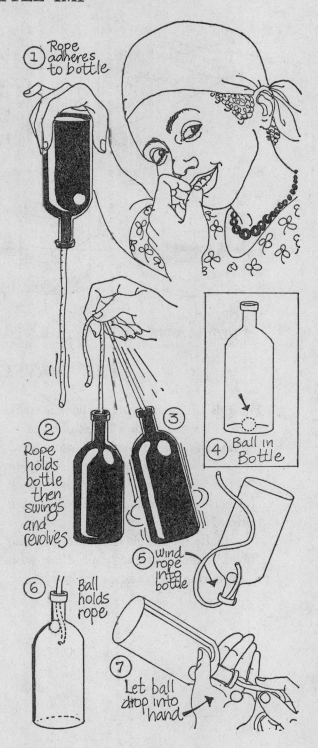

1. Rope adheres to bottle
2. Rope holds bottle then swings and revolves
3.
4. Ball in Bottle
5. wind rope into bottle
6. Ball holds rope
7. Let ball drop into hand

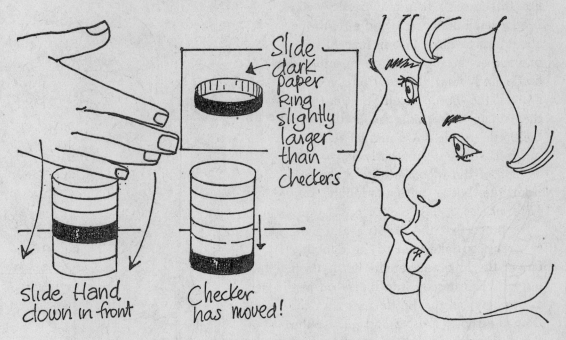

Slide dark paper Ring slightly larger than checkers

Slide Hand down in front

Checker has moved!

THE TRAVELING CHECKER

For this bit of deception show a stack of red checkers with a black checker in the middle. Form your hand into a loose fist and slide it down the stack. When you remove your hand the black checker has mysteriously traveled to the bottom!

Actually all the checkers are red. The "black" checker is simply a red one with a loose ring of black paper around it.

Your hand actually slides the paper ring to the bottom of the stack. You can then pocket the checkers after the trick; then, as an afterthought, pass them around for examination, since you have a real black checker in your pocket to pass out with the reds. With a bit of flair and showmanship, this trick will be able to catch even the most sophisticated audience.

THE MYSTIC BANANA

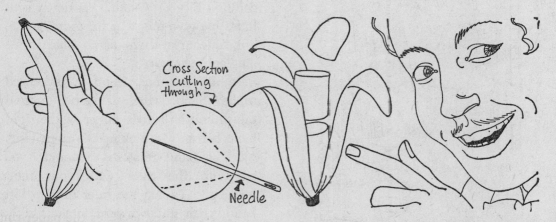

Cross Section
– cutting
through →

Needle

A real banana is used for this mystery. Hold the banana upright in your hand to show your audience that it is an ordinary banana. When you peel the banana it will fall apart in three pieces as though it were already cut!

A little deft preparation is required for this stunt. First, insert a needle through one segment line of the banana peel. Next, move the needle sideways, being careful not to pierce through the other sides of the banana. This cuts the banana but leaves no mark when the needle is removed. Make one more insertion to make three portions. No one will be able to tell that the banana had been prepared.

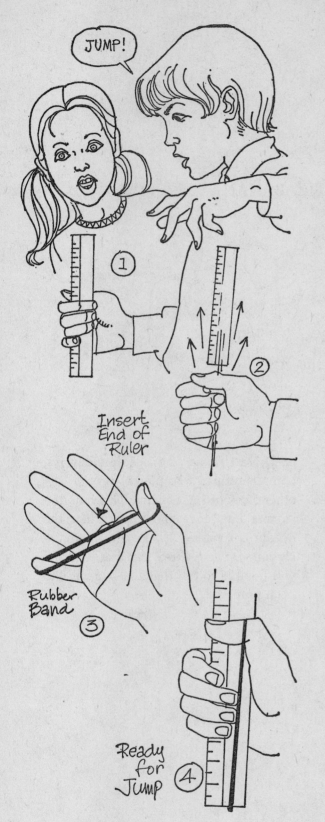

THE JUMPING RULER

A quick trick, good for several repeats and winding up with a surprise finish. A standard twelve-inch ruler, gripped in the right fist, rises several inches at your command; and each time you push it down with the left hand, it rises again in the same mysterious fashion (Fig. 1). Finally, at the order "Jump!" it takes off completely and springs almost to the ceiling (Fig. 2). Catching it deftly as it falls, you give the ruler for examination, but of course there is no clue to its magical behavior.

It all depends upon a fair-sized rubber band, which is looped around the thumb and little finger of the right hand before you pick up the ruler (Fig. 3). The band remains unseen as you point to the ruler with your right forefinger. Taking the ruler in your left hand, push it downward in your right fist, pressing its end into the lower strand of the rubber band, finally closing the right fist tightly when the ruler is about halfway down (Fig. 4).

By keeping the right hand slightly in motion, the stretched band will not be noticed, and when the right fist relaxes pressure, the ruler will rise, halting as you tighten your fist. A downward push by the left hand enables you to repeat the rise until you relax all pressure, when the ruler will zoom up toward the ceiling. Even after the jump, you can pick up the ruler with your left hand and begin all over, ending with a bigger jump, but at the finish, the right hand can drop the rubber band to the floor while the left hand passes the ruler around for inspection.

200

THE MAGIC MARK

With a burned match, make a slanted mark on the palm of your left hand, just below the little finger (Fig. 1). Let everyone see it there; then turn your hand palm downward, close your fist, and make a similar mark on the back of your hand (Fig. 2). Rub out the mark, turn your hand upward, open it, and to everyone's surprise, the rubbed-out mark will be seen crossing the mark originally there (Fig. 3).

Follow the directions precisely as given and the trick will work itself. Since the first mark crosses a crease in the palm, the mere closing of the hand causes it to make a duplicate impression at an opposite angle, so two marks appear when you open your hand.

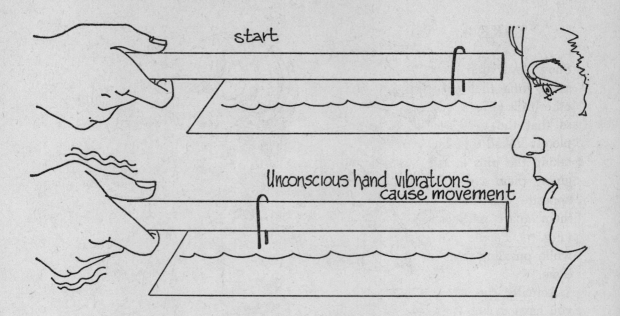

start

Unconscious hand vibrations cause movement

THE ANIMATED HAIRPIN

This is a walking hairpin. Just place an ordinary hairpin over one end of a ruler. Hold the other end of the ruler in your hand. Lower the ruler horizontally so that the dangling ends of the hairpin just touch the top of a smooth-surface table. YOUR HAND MUST NEVER TOUCH THE TABLE. Automatically the hairpin will walk the length of the ruler until it reaches your hand. Tip the ruler lightly and the hairpin will walk back.

This acrobatic performance of the hairpin is due to the unconscious vibration of your hand.

TAKE-APART PINS

Show everyone two ordinary large safety pins; then close one and link the other to it (Fig. 1). Now close that one, so that the two are firmly and completely linked together (Fig. 2). But on taking the pins at the lower ends and giving them a sliding, twisting pull in opposite directions, you actually take them apart without unclasping them (Fig. 3). People may examine the pins while puzzling over how the trick was done.

Actually, the action is automatic, but you have to know the secret and practice it a few times so you can do it without hesitation. To start, lay each pin on the table with its loose bar to the left. Clasp one pin shut; then take the other and thrust its upper end over the solid bar of the first pin; then under the loose bar of the first pin (as in Fig. 1).

Now close the loose bar of the second pin and clasp it shut, so that the bar lies above both bars of the first pin. This locks the pins firmly and legitimately together (as shown in Fig. 2). You are then all set to go. Grip the small ends of the pins between the thumb and fingers of each hand and draw them apart, keeping them flat but twisting them slightly and widening the angle as required (Fig. 4). This pulls the loose bars downward so they slip apart, but clasp themselves as they come free (as in Fig. 3).

NOTE: This can be done at any time with any safety pins, provided their loose bars are not too stiff. It also makes a great follow-up to Link the Pins (page 204), provided the pins are set in the correct position to be unlinked as just described.

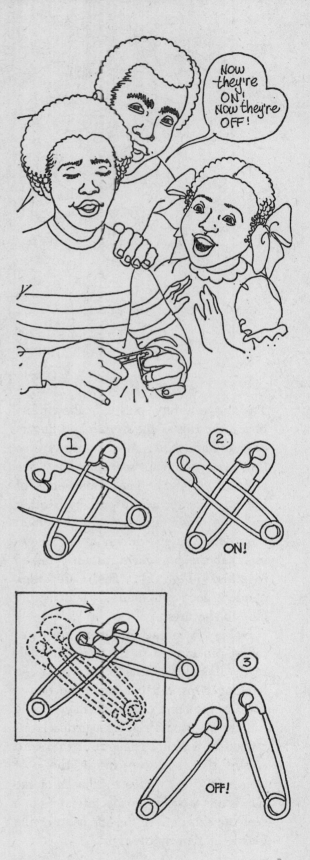

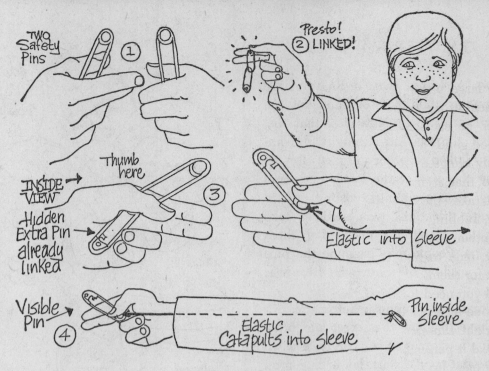

LINK THE PINS

Two large safety pins are shown between the tips of the thumb and fingers of each hand, the pins being upward so that everyone can see that they are clasped (Fig. 1). The upper ends of the pins are turned toward each other and the ends are brought together, then immediately drawn apart, showing that the pins have instantly linked together (Fig. 2). They are then handed for examination, leaving no clue to the mystery.

Unknown to the observers, an extra safety pin is used in the trick. It is already linked to the pin shown at the left fingertips, but it hangs head downward in the bend of the left fingers. The pin shown at the right fingertips is attached to a six-inch length of thin cord elastic that runs up inside the coat sleeve (Fig. 3). Since the backs of the hands are toward the spectators, no one sees the extra pin in the left hand or the elastic hidden by the right.

Thus prepared, you show the original pins at your fingertips (as in Fig. 1) and bring your hands together. No actual switch of pins is necessary, for the moment that they meet, the right hand lets its pin go and simply draws the visible pin from the left hand, bringing the extra pin to the tips of the left thumb and fingers. People see two separate pins to start and two linked pins at the finish; hence they never suspect the quick change that occurred.

NOTE: The cord elastic is put through the loop at the bottom of the right-hand pin and tied in a tight knot. The other end of the elastic is knotted to a smaller safety pin (Fig. 4), which is fastened well up the sleeve so that the big pin dangles just above the wrist, where the left hand can reach up and draw it down to the right thumb and fingers before taking its own linked pins from the pocket to begin the trick.

CLING-O-CLIPS

Two large paper clips of "jumbo" size are held at the tip of thumb and second finger of each hand, where they are rubbed gently together until one mysteriously clings to the other (Fig. 1). To prove that it must be magic, the left hand takes the clinging clips from the right, rubbing them apart (Fig. 2), so that other people can take the clips and try it, only to find that the trick won't work for them.

All you need for this near miracle is a tiny one-inch bar magnet, held between the right thumb and forefinger, which conceal it perfectly (Fig. 3). When you bring one clip in contact with the magnet, it also becomes magnetic, which gives it the power to attract the other clip (as in Fig. 1). But when the left hand draws both clips away, they come apart (as in Fig. 2), because the right-hand clip lacks the required power once it loses contact with the hidden magnet.

The demonstration can be repeated several times, always working for the performer but no one else; and at the finish, the clips can be dropped in the right coat pocket, the magnet going along with them.

To build up the effect for a group audience, you can use a few dozen paper clips, making one pair cling; then another and another, handing them out so everybody can try it.

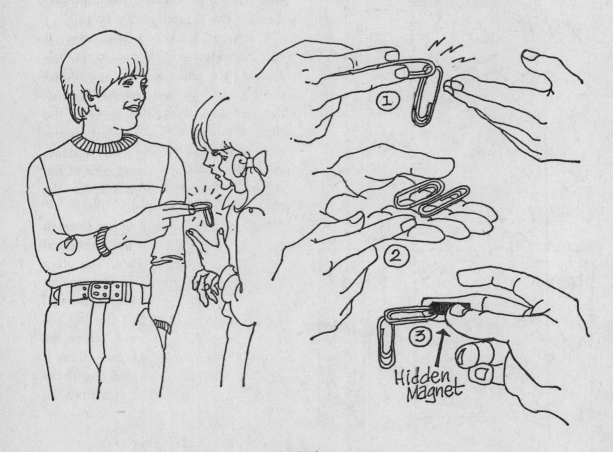

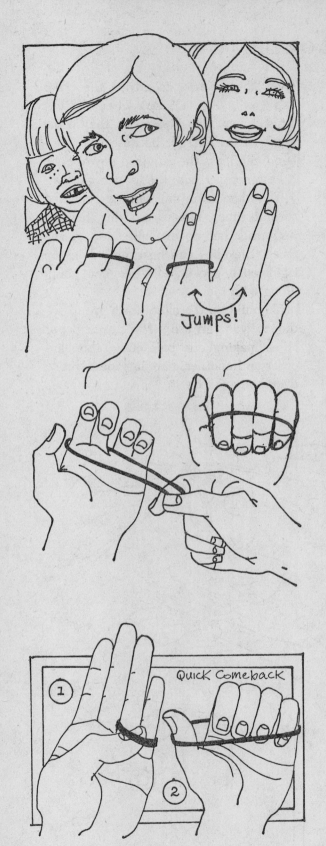

Jumps!

Quick Comeback

1
2

JUMPING ELASTIC

No magician's repertoire would be complete without the jumping elastic. Start by showing a rubber band around the first two fingers of your left hand. Use your right hand to snap the elastic, proving that it is tightly in position. Bend your fingers inward, letting everyone see the elastic around the first two fingers. Suddenly, extend your fingers and magically the rubber band jumps to the last two fingers of the hand!

The actual trickery begins when you snap the elastic with your right hand. Holding the palm of your left hand toward you, draw out the rubber band; then bend your fingers, inserting all of them into the loop thus formed. Turning your left hand so only the back is seen, the elastic shows apparently on the first two fingers only. A quick extension of the fingers and the rubber band jumps.

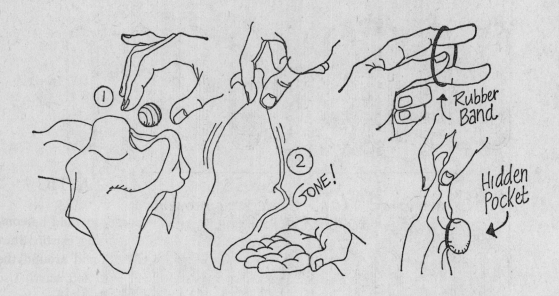

VANISHED BALL

For a quick vanish of a small ball, this is both easy and puzzling. Spread a handkerchief over your left hand so your right forefinger can poke a pocket down between the left thumb and fingers; then drop or push the ball into the pocket and close the handkerchief, stating that the ball will disappear! (Fig. 1). The right hand then grips a corner of the handkerchief, gives it a shake, and the ball is gone! (Fig. 2).

All you need is a tight rubber band, doubled around the left thumb and first two fingers, which are hidden beneath the handkerchief. Push the ball deep in the pocket and let the rubber band close above it. After shaking the handkerchief, the ball will stay safely hidden in back. Use a colored handkerchief with a fancy design and no one will see the pocket.

Instead of a small ball, you can vanish a large marble, a large coin, a thimble, or various other objects.

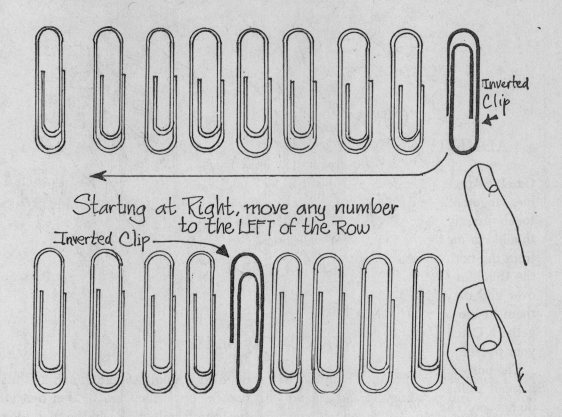

Inverted Clip

Starting at Right, move any number to the LEFT of the Row

Inverted Clip

MOVE THE CLIPS

Lay several paper clips in a row on the table. Ask somebody to move some clips one by one from one end of the row to the other. This is done while you turn your back or leave the room. When you come back to the table and touch the clips or just pass your hand over them, you immediately name the number moved.

One clip gives you the clue. It is at the right end of the row. Before you turn your back, specify that the clips must be moved from right to left. This last right-end clip is placed so that its long end is opposite those of the others —a detail that no one notices. After the clips are moved you simply count from the left end of the row, including the inverted clip, which tells you the number moved.

ADHESIVE THIMBLES

Carefully press the mouths of two thimbles together. Make sure their rims touch exactly. Tilt them so that one thimble is on top. Release your fingers from the bottom thimble. Miraculously, the thimbles stick together! Turn them over and they still stick together! Toss them in the air and they still stick together! Catch them and put them in your pocket.

The unseen prop that does the trick is a small rubber ball that the spectators do not see. The ball is just a trifle larger than the interior of the thimbles. To prepare the thimbles first wedge the ball into one thimble. Keeping the ball away from view, press the thimbles mouth to mouth. Both thimbles cling to the ball, which is hidden between them.

MAGNETIC MATCHES

Lay two safety matches on a table, keeping the heads in one direction. State that when you draw your forefinger between them, a magnetic force will drive them apart. As you draw your finger between them they actually fly apart as you predicted.

To work this trick all you have to do is put your head close to the table, breathe lightly on the table at the right moment as you draw your finger between the matches, and they will move apart.

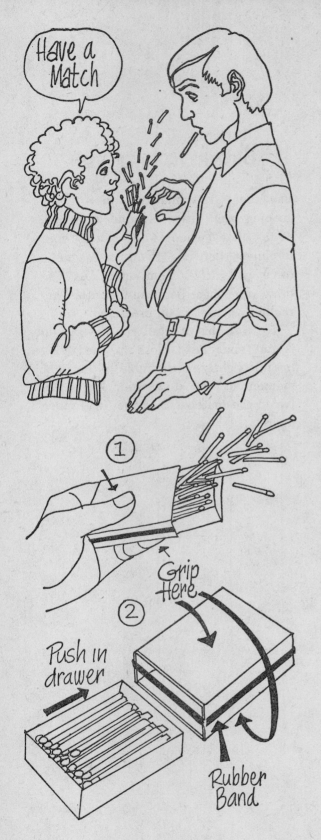

HAVE A MATCH

This is a good opener to any tricks involving matches. An ordinary box of safety matches is offered to a spectator with the casual comment, "Have a match." As he reaches for the closed box, it suddenly springs open, ejecting half a dozen matches in his direction (Fig. 1).

The trick is provided by a dark rubber band, which you gird around the sides and ends of the matchbox cover. You then push the drawer into the cover from the outer end and grip the inner end of the cover, with your thumb on top and fingers beneath (Figs. 1 and 2). Have this set beforehand, and when you extend the matchbox and release pressure, it will fly open as described. If you remove the drawer with your left hand and dump the matches on the table, you will have ample opportunity to lower your right hand and detach the rubber hand, letting it fall unnoticed.

QUICK MATCHBOX VANISH

Facing the audience, hold a closed matchbox projecting upward from your left fist; then cup your right hand above the matchbox and thrust it downward. Then, turning to your left, raise your left hand, point to it with your right forefinger, spread your left hand wide, and the box is gone! Moments later, you reach beneath the table or into your coat pocket and bring out the missing matchbox.

Only a small amount of skill is needed for this neat surprise. As you press downward with your cupped right hand, press forward as well, so that the matchbox, instead of going down into the left fist, is tilted flat on the knuckle of the left forefinger, unseen by the viewers. This enables you to retain the matchbox in the bend of your right fingers; and by turning the back of your right hand toward the spectators, the matchbox remains concealed there while you point toward your left hand with your right forefinger.

After the box "vanishes" from the left hand, the right hand can bring it back as described.

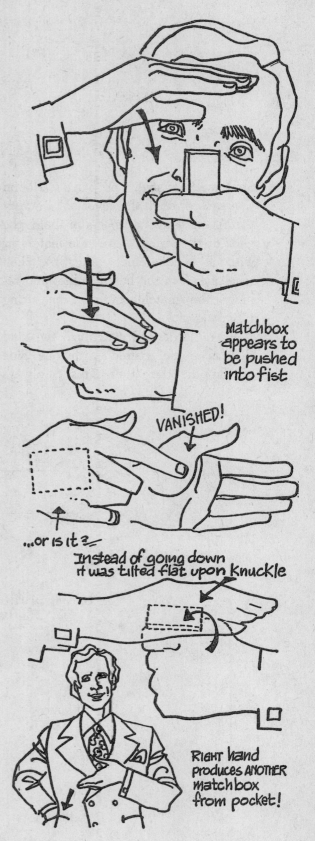

Matchbox appears to be pushed into fist

VANISHED!

...or is it?

Instead of going down it was tilted flat upon knuckle

Right hand produces ANOTHER matchbox from pocket!

STRING AND MATCHBOX

Start with a string or narrow ribbon that runs through the cover of an empty matchbox. Have a spectator hold the ends of the string. Cover the matchbox with a handkerchief (Fig. 1), then reach beneath the handkerchief and remove the matchbox from the string (Fig. 2).

Use a cardboard matchbox, the kind that is manufactured with one side overlapping the other. This is always one of the narrow sides. To prepare the box, pry that side apart. Apply a piece of double-sided Scotch tape to one side of this flap and press these two side pieces together loosely. The matchbox can be inspected, if you wish. Beneath the handkerchief you merely open the side of the cover, take the matchbox from the string, and press its sides gently together. The box may then be shown free of the string.

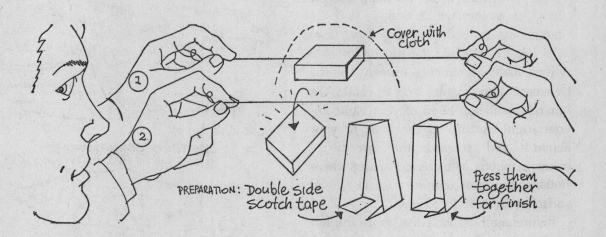

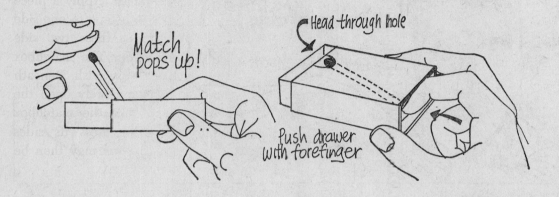

Match pops up!

Head through hole

Push drawer with forefinger

POP-UP MATCH

A lone match provides the surprise in this neat introductory effect. Bring a box of matches from your pocket with your right hand; wave your fingers above it, and as the drawer obligingly opens a match pops up from the box. Retrieve the match with your left hand, and offer the match for examination.

Beforehand, prepare the matchbox by making a small hole in the top of the cover, a quarter inch from the outer end. Close the box and push the lone match in through the hole until only the head protrudes. By secretly pushing the drawer open with your right forefinger, you automatically pop the match into sight, enabling the left hand to pluck it free before anyone realizes that it came up through the cover.

213

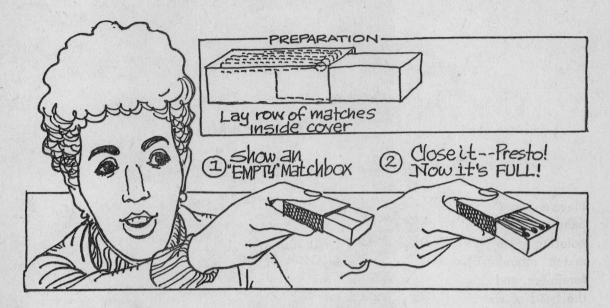

Lay row of matches
inside cover

① Show an "EMPTY" Matchbox

② Close it--Presto!
Now it's FULL!

MATCHES FROM NOWHERE

Show a small matchbox with its drawer well extended so that everyone can see that it is completely empty. Push the box shut, then open it, and the drawer is practically filled with matches that seemingly came from nowhere!

For this trick use a matchbox with a shallow drawer and trim about one-sixteenth inch from the upper edge of the drawer, all the way around. Lay a row of matches inside the cover of the box, and push the drawer into the cover and well out the other end, wedging the matches in place. Then adjust them so that none show.

Hold the box with its top side upward, showing the empty drawer. Push the drawer shut with your fingers, while your thumb blocks the other end to prevent the matches from coming out. Instead, they drop into the drawer; and when you push it open, the matches put in their appearance, almost filling the shallow drawer.

TURNABOUT MATCH

Place a paper match on the outspread palm of the left hand, with its head pointing toward your thumb. Cover the match momentarily with your right forefinger, and when you lift the finger, the head of the match has turned the other way!

Prepare for this trick by splitting a paper match lengthwise and peeling the two portions apart, heads and all. Then reverse one and glue the two together. Lay the match on your left palm with a head showing to the left; and a slight sidewise pressure from the extended right forefinger will turn the match over, so the head will apparently do a turnabout. This can be repeated over and over with the same baffling result.

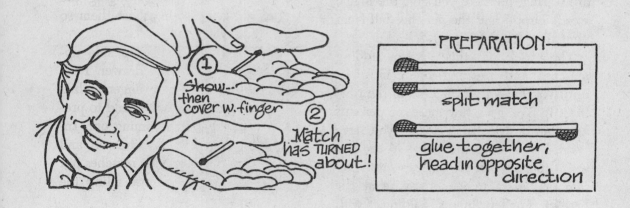

① Show... then cover w. finger

② Match has TURNED about!

PREPARATION

split match

glue together, head in opposite direction

MAGNETIC MATCHES

Use large-sized kitchen safety matches for this magical effect, either taking them from the box as you need them, or from a large pile lying on the table. Start by taking matches with the left hand and laying them on the right palm, so that they form a row at an angle between the right thumb and fingers (Fig. 1). Pause to press the matches tightly in position with the left fingers (Fig. 2) and then add a few more to the row. Do this again, adding more matches from the box or pile, continuing to press the growing row (as in Figs. 1 and 2).

While still pressing the matches, turn both hands over so the right hand is back upward. Draw the left hand away, showing it empty, but the matches remain in the right hand, as though magnetized there (Fig. 3). While people are staring, puzzled, you give the magic word "Drop!" and the matches fall from your right hand (Fig. 4).

The trick is this: Keep adding matches and pressing them in place until you have eight or nine in the row. Start to pick up a few more, or perhaps add one or two; then decide you have enough and leave the extras in the box or on the pile. In so doing, secretly retain one extra match crosswise at the base of your left fingers, holding it with the thumb (Fig. 5).

In giving the row a final press (as in Fig. 2), grip the ends of the extra match between the base of the right thumb and little finger so that it wedges the row in place (Fig. 6). The hands can now be turned over and the left

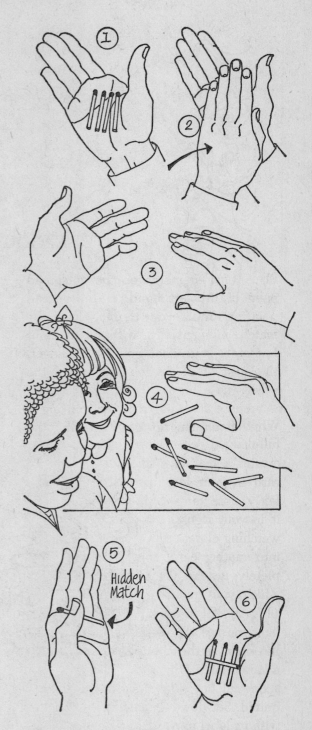

drawn away, with the right retaining the "magnetized" matches (Fig. 3) until they are allowed to drop by spreading the right fingers (Fig. 4).

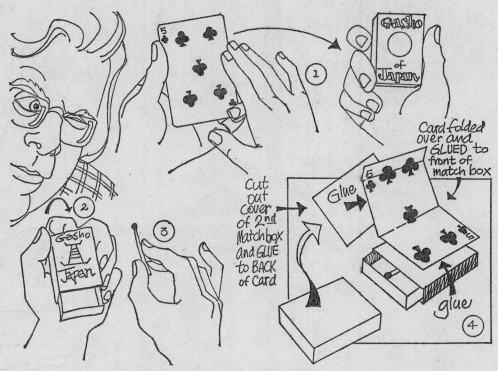

Card folded over and GLUED to front of match box

Glue

Cut out cover of 2nd Matchbox and GLUE to BACK of Card

glue

CARD TO MATCHBOX

Whether shown as a quick puzzler or a full-fledged effect, this trick usually creates a real surprise. Hold a playing card in your left hand, showing it at fairly close range, and apparently take it in your right hand (Fig. 1). People watching closely expect to see it change into another card, or even vanish completely; instead, it becomes a matchbox, which you transfer to your left hand (Fig. 2). All in the same action, the left hand pushes the drawer of the matchbox open, so the right hand can take out a loose match (Fig. 3).

Special but simple preparation is required. Set down a matchbox crosswise with its label upward, and on it glue the lower section of a bridge-sized playing card, face up. The card must be fitted exactly to the cover of the box; therefore the edges of the card may require a slight trimming. Now fold the loose portion of the card downward across the label and continue with a further fold over the side of the box (Fig. 4). With the card folded down, take the label and side from another matchbox and glue them to the back of the card, again making an exact fit.

You are now ready. Show the card with its loose end extended upward between thumb and fingertips of the left hand (as in Fig. 1), with the matchbox concealed in the bend of the left fingers. The right hand covers the card and folds it down over the matchbox, while the right thumb helps turn the box bottom upward. Now you bring the label side of the matchbox into view, transferring it to the left hand, which grips the sides of the box between thumb and second finger so that the forefinger can push the drawer open (as in Fig. 3).

CHAPTER TEN: Special Tricks for a Complete Act

Howard Thurston

OVER A PERIOD OF twenty-five years, Howard Thurston toured the United States season after season, with the largest, most elaborate, and most profitable magic show of all time, requiring more than thirty people and two railway baggage cars—or more—to carry his equipment. Between tours, Thurston and his assistants constructed new illusions in his own workshop, which was equipped with a stage to try them out. Huge posters depicted these new wonders to attract old patrons to the theaters in cities where Thurston appeared regularly, and it has been estimated that during his career, he spent half a million dollars on that form of advertising alone.

The older equipment was stored in warehouses in Whitestone, Long Island, where Thurston's workshop was located, and he and his family spent the summers on a sizable estate. By the time Thurston had expanded his show to the point where he played only the largest theaters in the biggest cities, he had enough equipment in storage to create two other full evening shows besides his own. And Thurston did exactly that.

One of these shows was headed by Dante, a magician of long standing, who was booked in cities where Thurston had formerly appeared. The other, Tampa, started with a smaller show, but later took over Dante's route, after Dante went to South America. Still later, Thurston's brother Harry went on tour with a large tent show featuring many of Thurston's best illusions.

This was truly magic on a grand scale, yet it all stemmed from a very small beginning. Back around 1900, Thurston was doing a card

act in small-time vaudeville. When he went to England, hoping to get bookings there, his act became a sensation and he used all his profits to build a stage show, which he took on a world tour. He made enough money from his stage show to close a deal with Kellar, then America's leading magician, who was about ready to retire. As Kellar's successor, Thurston went on to still greater fame; but always, his card act was retained as a feature of his big show.

The act began with skilled manipulations in which Thurston vanished cards one by one, showed his hand empty, back and front, then reproduced the missing cards at his fingertips. This formed a prototype that later performers, like Cardini, were to develop further. Following those manipulations, Thurston presented his version of the Rising Cards, one of the oldest tricks in magic, to which he had added a new twist that took the London audiences by storm. In the original version, a pack of cards was placed in a glass, and one by one, chosen cards rose from the pack and toppled onto the table. But Thurston held the pack upright in his left hand, raised his right hand a few feet above it, and snapped his fingers in command, whereupon a card rose majestically through the air, to be received by the hand above. This was repeated by succeeding cards in the same mysterious fashion, and Thurston concluded his act by throwing cards to the audience, even to spectators in the highest balcony.

While Thurston was in England, he met a writer named William Hilliar, who suggested that they put out a book explaining Thurston's card tricks. Thurston agreed, because although his act was distinctly his own, some of his manipulations were already being used by other card workers. But he hesitated when it came to the Rising Cards, because it was designed strictly for the stage and depended on a long thread operated by a concealed assistant. So he thought up a substitute that could be worked anywhere.

At that time, stores were selling self-coiling measuring tapes that could be pulled from a small, cylindrical box, then drawn back rapidly by releasing a spring. Instead of a tape measure, Thurston suggested a long black thread, with a button on the outer end, provided with a dab of wax that could be pressed against the back of a card, causing it to rise from the pack when the spring was released. Since the book was ready to go to press, this untried idea was given as the explanation to the Rising Cards, on the assumption that it probably would work if someone took the trouble to make it up.

Instead, the book reached America ahead of Thurston, and when he arrived, magic dealers had already made up the "card reel," as they called it, and were selling it as Thurston's Rising Cards to amateur magicians who had never seen Thurston's stage presentation but who were quite satisfied with the close-range version.

As time went by, the trick was simplified to the point where even the reel was unnecessary, so that now you can perform the close-range card rise with the simplest of items and a few minutes of preparation, as follows:

Take a thin black thread, twelve inches or more in length, and wind one end tightly around an ordinary pin, which you attach to the lapel of your jacket, or to the jacket itself. To the other end of the thread fix a dab of beeswax or some other slightly sticky substance—such as chewing gum—and twist it so the thread becomes firmly imbedded in the wax. Attach the wax to the back of a button on your jacket.

Have a card selected and bring it to the top of the pack by any of the methods used for that purpose. Hold the pack upright in your left hand, fingers in front, thumb in back, running across the pack. With your right hand, pluck the wax from the button and press it against the back of the chosen card. Turn away as you do this, in order to take a new position farther from the spectators. That action helps you to fix the wax without anyone noticing it. Now, facing your audience again, extend the pack about six inches forward from your body and bring your right hand upward in back of the pack so that your thumb engages the thread, which is hanging loosely between the lapel of your jacket and the pack.

As the thread becomes taut, move the hand more rapidly upward and forward, causing the card to zoom up to the waiting right hand, which plucks it from the air as the thread shortens. The fact that the card moves forward as it rises is not noticed, as it comes directly toward the onlookers, giving the impression that the right hand is simply reaching for the rising card. The right hand displays the card with fingers in front and thumb in back. This makes it easy for the right thumb to detach the wax pellet while the hand places the card at the front of the pack.

Always, when performing this version of the Rising Cards, you should wear a dark jacket or sweater, so the thread will not be seen. After finishing the trick, it can be allowed to dangle until you have an opportunity to turn away and regain the wax pellet, which you can then press back on the button where it was originally.

When performing for a fair-sized group, the effect can be increased by having three or more people select cards and having them rise successively from the pack. To do this, all the selected cards are brought to the top of the pack. Then, after making the first card rise, bring your forefinger in back of it, so that when you detach the wax pellet, you can retain it between the tips of your right thumb and forefinger. Thus, after putting the first card at the front of the pack, you can secretly press the pellet onto the next card, at the back of the pack. This enables you to repeat the rise with the second card; and you can apply the same procedure to the third card, finally letting the pellet drop and dangle unnoticed.

COLOR-CHANGING BALLOON

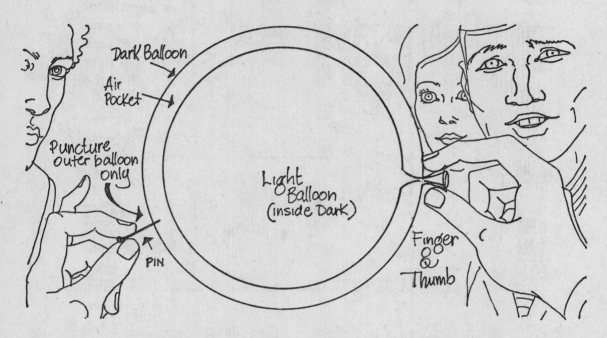

Hold an inflated dark-colored balloon with your fingertips. Be sure everyone sees the color. Lightly point and touch the balloon with your other hand; then presto, the balloon changes color! To do this, put a light-colored balloon inside a dark one. Inflate both together, then spread the stem of the dark balloon so you can inflate it further, forming an air pocket between them. While your left hand draws attention to the balloon, your right hand pierces the dark balloon with a concealed pin. The balloon will burst! Be careful that you pierce only the dark outside balloon.

RESTORED PAPER STRIP

Show the audience that your hands are absolutely empty. Pick up a piece of paper twelve inches or so long. Tear it in half. While your audience watches closely, crumple the torn pieces; then slowly pull out the full-length strip, entirely restored!

The secret is simple. You must use crepe paper, which stretches to twice its length. You actually tear the paper in half, but when you crumple it, retain one half in your left hand. As you draw out the other half with your right fingers your left fingers hold that end firmly to make the paper stretch, all the time keeping the crumpled piece hidden, so the left hand can pocket it later.

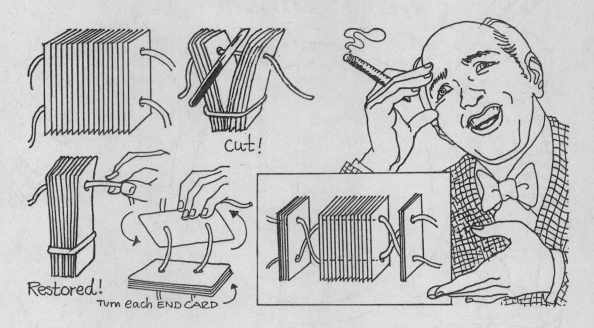

For this effect, you need a few dozen playing cards, with holes punched through them about three-quarters inch from each end; these can easily be made with a standard punch. Through each series of holes, run a ribbon about two feet in length, so that both ribbons can be drawn freely back and forth. After demonstrating this, give someone a choice of either ribbon and then wrap the other ribbon around its end of the pack, tying it in a knot. The end with the chosen ribbon is pointed upward, so that you can cut that ribbon between the cards.

Having done that with a pair of scissors, give the upper end of the pack a sharp snap or a quick riffle and promptly draw the ribbon back and forth, completely restored! For a complete convincer, you can actually pull the ribbon completely through the pack and offer it for inspection to prove that it is actually restored.

Before showing the trick, hold the pack flat and give a few top cards a half turn horizontally. Turn the pack over and do the same with the bottom cards. This causes the ribbons to cross, so that each supplants the other near the center of the pack, but when you draw on the ribbons they seem to run straight through. Therefore, when you are apparently cutting the top ribbon, you are really cutting the bottom ribbon. This makes the "restoration" automatic and allows you to draw the top ribbon free at the finish.

NOTE: Any type of game cards, or even blank cards, may be punched with holes and used instead of playing cards.

SILLY SPOOKS

For a weird party stunt, this is unquestionably the greatest, because you can play it straight and baffle everybody, or you can clown it and let everyone in on the fun.

On a table, set out the following items: a small bell, a twelve-inch ruler, an inflated toy balloon, a pair of dice, and a pack of playing cards. Then spread a large silk handkerchief between your hands, so that it hides all the articles. That done, state that you will put the spooks to work!

The bell rings and comes flying over the outspread silk. The ruler waves itself above the top; then drops from sight; and up comes the toy balloon, followed by the dice and a shower of playing cards (Fig. 1). That's when you whisk away the cloth and take a bow,

letting the spooks accept all the applause. Here is how it works:

On the upper right corner of the cloth, fix a small hook or hooked clamp. Stand with your right side toward the table, as if to stretch your right arm in front of it (Fig. 2). Then, in order to gain better coverage, bring your right hand to your left shoulder, make a right turn toward the table, and extend your left hand with its corner of the cloth (Fig. 3). By hooking the right corner to your left coat sleeve, you gain full coverage for the manifestations (see Fig. 1).

Your right hand, being free, dips behind the cloth and does all the work in rapid style (Fig. 4), finally coming up to the left shoulder, regaining its corner of the cloth as you step away.

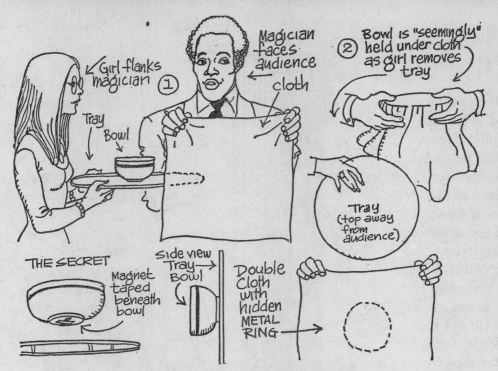

THE VANISHING BOWL

This is a great effect for your next magic show! Begin by displaying an ornamental bowl measuring six or more inches across and three or more inches deep, while your assistant is bringing you a metal tray with a large cloth lying on it. Place the bowl on the tray, cover it, and lift the bowl beneath the cloth, while your assistant lowers the tray and steps away. As you approach the audience, give the cloth a sudden toss in the air and catch it as it falls, showing both sides to prove that the bowl has completely vanished!

To perform this trick use a light plastic bowl of the type that delicatessens use to sell salads. Take two small but powerful alnico magnets, obtainable at many hardware stores, and tape them beneath the bowl. Form a wire ring the size of the bowl rim and place it between two large handkerchiefs or similar cloths, hemming their borders together; you will be ready to proceed.

Show the bowl and set it on the tray, where the magnets will hold it firmly. Spread the cloth over the bowl, fitting the wire ring to the rim. As you lift the bowl, the assistant naturally lowers the tray by releasing one hand and dropping one edge of the tray downward, so that the spectators see only the bottom of the tray. This enables your assistant to walk off, carrying the bowl unseen behind the tray. You then step forward and "vanish" the bowl by letting the hidden ring slide down into a corner of the double cloth.

If you want, you can have the plastic cover of the bowl lying beneath the cloth at the start. That will enable you to pour water into the bowl before setting it on the tray. Then by lifting the cover under the cloth, you can clamp it on the bowl through the cloth and later shift the cloth to bring the hidden ring into position for the vanish. This takes more practice, but adds to the effect.

BALL AND ROPE

Here is a striking effect that can be performed as part of a juggling act or used in a full-fledged magic show. In either case, it is best when worked with an assistant who can help speed the action and avoid any false starts or delays.

Show a smooth rope about a yard in length and stretch it from hand to hand, keeping it taut and level, while your helper places a lightweight ball on it.

Not only does the ball balance there, which is remarkable in itself, but also, as you tilt the rope, the ball runs along it back and forth, finally being plucked from the rope by the helpful assistant.

Although this takes some practice, it is a lot easier than it looks. It depends on a white thread, a little shorter than the rope, which you tie close to each end of the rope, where the thread stays unnoticed. When you draw the rope taut, bring the thread in back and thrust your thumbs straight upward between the rope and the thread, so that the two form a hidden track. The assistant places a light ball—preferably of plastic—on the track, and with careful tilts, you can run it back and forth as often as you want.

You can work it alone by holding the ball between the tips of your right thumb and fingers, easing it toward the track as you tilt the rope toward the left and catching the ball on its return—but it is faster and easier when an assistant helps.

Rope

Thread

THE ORIENTAL
SNOWSTORM

This is a neat, surprising mystery, suitable for parlor or platform. Take some strips of white tissue paper and soak them in a bowl of water. Now squeeze them into a wad, and hold it in one hand while you pick up a small fan with the other. As you fan the wadded tissue, it not only becomes dry, it is also transformed into tiny bits of paper that fly about like miniature snowflakes!

Some simple preparation is needed for this effect. Beforehand, cut a quantity of tissue paper into tiny shreds and pile the "flakes" into a square of similar paper (see A under Preparation). Bring the corners up together (B) and put a

small rubber band around them to form a compact bundle (C), which is placed beneath several strips of tissue paper near the left front corner of the table.

Slightly to the right is a bowl or a glass of water, and behind it an oblong box, about three inches in height, or a stack of paperback books, serving as a stand, with a folding fan resting on it (D). You are then ready to proceed as follows:

Standing at the left of the table, pick up the strips of tissue paper with your right hand (Fig. 1), bringing the bundle along with it (Fig. 2). Transfer the strips and bundle to the left hand, which keeps the compact packet hidden in the bend of the fingers. At the same time the right hand draws away the strips, one or two at a time, and dunks them in the water (Fig. 3), squeezing them in turn until they form a tight wad. The right hand then moves toward the left and pretends to place the soaked wad in the left hand, actually retaining it in the right, while the left fingers open just enough for observers to glimpse the little bundle, mistaking it for the wadded strips (Fig. 4).

This is a very effective "switch," as observers think they see the wadded papers at all times, so only a slight amount of skill is needed and a little practice makes it perfect. While the left hand is drawing attention in its direction, the right moves downward and picks up the fan, dropping the wad behind the box or stack of books (Fig. 5). This is facilitated by having the lower end of the fan projecting in back, making it natural to pick it up from there.

The right hand opens the fan and starts waving it beneath the left, which moves upward and downward in rhythmic fashion. This enables the left thumb and fingers to slip the rubber band from the little bundle, which can be torn open to release the paper snowflakes (Fig. 6). As the spectators watch the increasing flurry swirl upward, it is a simple matter to roll the torn covering into a tiny ball, which can be dropped unnoticed to the floor, while lowering the left hand.

By having a handkerchief lying on the table, you can wipe your empty hands after the snowstorm and use the handkerchief to cover the wadded paper while you remove the box or books. Later the handkerchief can be picked up and pocketed, taking the wad along with it.

THE INEXHAUSTIBLE BOX

Ever since the top-hat era, the mysterious production of silk handkerchiefs and various other items has been popular in many magic shows. Since top hats have long been out of style, inexhaustible boxes have replaced them; and here is a type so simple and practical that it can be made up on very short notice at practically no cost. Any squarish cardboard box will do, but instead of a tight-fitting lid, the box should have a loose square of heavy cardboard for a cover.

At the start, the box is seen resting on a table, with the cardboard square lying flat on top of it. The square projects from all sides, since its measurements are purposely made greater than those of the box. Begin by tilting the front edge of the square upward and backward, so that when it reaches a vertical position, you can turn or twirl it around, showing that both sides are completely free of any deception (Fig. 1). With a forward, downward tilt, you again show the other side of the cardboard square and hold it vertically in one hand while you lift the box with your other hand, to show it totally empty (Fig. 2).

That done, put the box back on the table and flop the square flat on top, just as it was at the start. Showing both hands empty and drawing your sleeves so high that it would be impossible to sneak anything from them, make a few mystic waves. Then, slowly, lift the front edge of the lid upward and backward with both hands, carrying it clear across and turning that same edge down in back of the box, clearly showing both sides of the square during the turnover. Dipping your empty hands into the box, begin pulling out silks and other articles, such as ribbons, party streamers, plastic drinking glasses, Chinese lanterns, and various toys or ornaments, a whole magic boxload!

All you need besides the lid, the box, and the load are a few large, thin rubber bands and several inches of black thread, the exact length being determined by a preliminary trial. One end of the thread is tied to a rubber band; the other is tied through a hole near the edge of the cardboard lid, at point A as opposed to the opposite edge, B. Nest the drinking glasses, pack them with various items, and wrap the silks around them, using the rubber

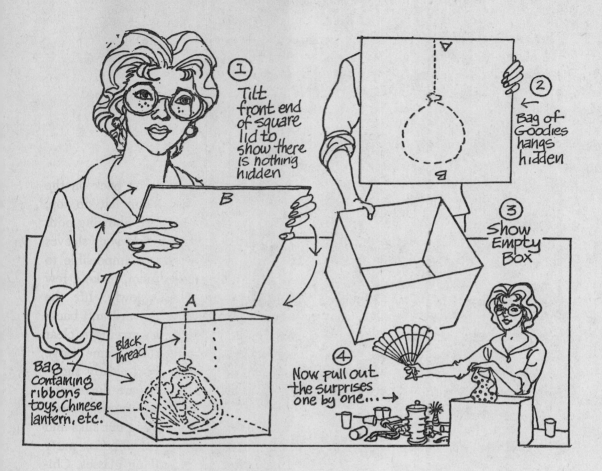

① Tilt front end of square lid to show there is nothing hidden

② Bag of Goodies hangs hidden

③ Show Empty Box

④ Now pull out the surprises one by one....→

Bag containing ribbons toys, Chinese lantern, etc.

Black Thread

bands to hold the entire load as compactly as possible.

Set the square so edge A is close to the rear rim of the box with the load dangling inside the box. Start by raising edge B upward so it can be shown with the load still in the box (Fig. 1). Then tilt B forward and downward over the front rim of the box. This brings A straight upward, so the load comes behind the square and is hidden while the other hand lifts the box and shows it empty (Fig. 2).

This move is reversed when the square is flopped on the box, putting the load inside again. Then, after showing the hands empty and rolling up the sleeves, tilt edge B upward, backward, and clear over the rear of the box, letting the square stand there while you reach into the box and release the rubber bands so that the load expands and can be produced item by item. Use dark paper for the interior of the box and dark strips of paper as ornamentation for the cardboard square, so the black thread cannot be noticed.